EMOTE

EMOTE

Using Emotions to Make Your Message Memorable

By Vikas Gopal Jhingran

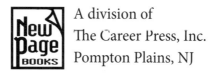

A division of
The Career Press, Inc.
Pompton Plains, NJ

EMOTE
EDITED BY ROGER SHEETY
TYPESET BY DIANA GHAZZAWI
Cover design by Howard Grossman/12E Design
Printed in the U.S.A.

To order this title, please call toll-free 1-800-CAREER-1 (NJ and Canada: 201-848-0310) to order using VISA or MasterCard, or for further information on books from Career Press.

The Career Press, Inc.
220 West Parkway, Unit 12
Pompton Plains, NJ 07444
www.careerpress.com
www.newpagebooks.com

Library of Congress Cataloging-in-Publication Data
CIP Data Available Upon Request.

This book is dedicated to my parents, Manoj Gopal Jhingran and Ranjana Jhingran. Their sacrifice and love have made it possible for me to write this book.

Acknowledgments

This book would not have been possible without the support of my wife, Anjali. She has been patient and supportive beyond my imagination. Be it reviewing the manuscript or giving additional time to two young children so that I can write, she is the reason I have been able to write this book.

I also want to thank my parents for their enthusiasm and support. Their excitement at my success is so pure and unconditional. It is wonderful to have them in my camp.

Several people at Shell helped along the way. Ram Gopalkrishnan provided valuable feedback that sparked several ideas. Similarly, Stephen Hodges started a chain of ideas around introverts and extraverts when he reviewed Susan Cain's book, *Quiet.* I thank Robert Patterson for taking the time to read the manuscript and provide comments on applicability of the concepts in business settings. I also thank Aamir Farid for his time and encouragement through the years. Discussions on verbal communication with Aamir helped energize and clarify many issues.

I thank my group of friends in Houston for the many discussions and endless support that they provided. I am sorry I could not fulfill your request to include a chapter called "Sex and Communication" to ensure huge sales of the book. Your craziness and support have helped me endure.

Special thanks to my literary agent, Anne Devlin, for having the courage to take on a first-time author. I hope every first-time author has a chance to work with an agent like Anne. She is responsive and supportive, yet practical. She did an outstanding job.

I also appreciate Career Press for their confidence in *Emote*. Their staff has been very helpful and encouraging.

A special thank you to Monica at RootSky Books for editing the book and helping me prepare a proposal. She laid a good foundation that helped me find a publisher.

I also want to thank Rice University for access to their libraries. I spent many weekends there poring over reference books and magazines. Their staff is always courteous and very helpful.

Contents

Introduction

In 2001, I was gainfully employed in the oil and gas industry in Houston, Texas. I worked with some very smart people in a small boutique engineering firm. We targeted a niche in the offshore oil and gas sector and were good at it. I enjoyed my work but was frequently irritated that I was not allowed to make presentations to clients on the work that I had performed. My manager and I often discussed this issue and he was candid with me: "Vikas, we don't get many opportunities to make these presentations. Under such circumstances, it's only appropriate that our best speaker and presenter stand up in front of potential clients."

I could not argue with this sentiment. I would do the same if I owned the company.

Instead, I decided to improve my presentation skills. I committed to becoming so good at presentations that it would be a disadvantage for my company not to let me stand up in front of clients. Over the next few months, I feverishly searched for courses and classes that could help me become a better speaker. I did not find many options.

After considerable research, I joined the Dale Carnegie Course. This was not a public speaking course per se, but a leadership course. However, it did have a speaking component built into it, and rightly so because verbal communication is an important aspect of leadership. The course required many short speeches, most of them only two minutes long. The first speech I made during the course was a two-minute talk introducing myself to the other class members. Even though I was supposed to talk about myself, I had prepared well. I had gone over the talk many times, written it out on a sheet of paper, and made sure I covered some key points.

Nothing, though, could have prepared me for what came next. When my turn came to speak, I was so nervous that my hands were shaking. I had brought notes with me, but they were useless because my hands were shaking so much that I could not read them. I finally decided to keep my hands in my pockets, knowing full well that I was not supposed to do that. However, I did not want my fellow classmates to notice my shaking hands. When I was done with my speech, I did not remember a word I had said. I was just happy that it was over.

This experience was eye-opening for me. It bothered me that I could be so scared of anything, let alone something as innocuous as speaking in front of people. Growing up in India, I had relatively few opportunities to make presentations. Though I did attend a high school with a very good debating team, I was not on it. Neither was I part of any forum that would allow me to get in front of people. Whenever I had some spare time, it was invested in working hard at math and science so that I could go to a good university in India. Speaking, communications, or even an interview, was not part of the selection process to get into an engineering university. All this ensured that in 2001 I found out that I was second to none in anything related to math, science, and engineering but was way behind on the communication and presentation aspects. No one had told me that this would matter in my professional growth.

From those humble beginnings, I worked hard and grew rapidly as a speaker during the three-month Dale Carnegie Course. After it was over, I continued to look for a forum to practice my speaking skills and came across Toastmasters International. This turned out to be a true blessing. Toastmasters clubs offer an ideal forum to hone and experiment with presentation techniques. From 2002 on, I got many opportunities to practice my speaking skills during Toastmasters club meetings, but more importantly, I got the opportunity to be around some very good speakers who helped and mentored me.

Hard work and perseverance paid off in 2007 when I won the World Championship of Public Speaking.

No Indian had done this before. In fact, I was only the second speaker of Asian origin to have won the World Championship in its 80-year history. The first, M. Arabella Bengson, was a Canadian citizen of Philippine origin who achieved the distinction in 1986.

The 2007 win was a unique achievement in many ways. My background did not fit the profile of a professional speaker. Most winners are extraverts and in professions that require them to be in front of people on a regular basis. They are in sales, some are ministers, and others have marketing, music, and theatre backgrounds. I had no background in any form of art. I was a numbers person, an introvert, trained at some of the most difficult technical universities in the world. Logic was my forte, not art. It really was a unique achievement.

By 2007, I had started to develop a unique approach to speaking. My speeches had strong emotional content and were delivered with profound messages that left a lasting impact on my audience. I was particularly careful about the emotions that I left with my audience—what I call the final emotion. This concept has now become a cornerstone of my speaking in recent years, and I discuss it extensively in this book. I have found that the core principles of the approach also apply to other forms of verbal communications like one-on-one conversation or in a small team setting.

My approach to verbal communication, and to public speaking in particular, is to understand the soul of a speech, master the mechanics of speaking, and use this information to connect on an emotional level with the audience.

This book is an attempt at sharing with you this approach. It is not a lecture on the "right" way to speak. It is only a different perspective on verbal communication and public speaking. Although many readers can benefit from the approach I share, my expectation is that this book will particularly help two groups of people: introverts and immigrants. I belong to both of these groups.

Introverts often feel uneasy while speaking in front of others. Interacting with people is not where they get their energy, and the very prospect of speaking before an audience is exhausting for them. Hence, introverts are exasperated when this is considered an important trait for leadership positions. Introverts will find my approach to speaking refreshing and enabling. They will appreciate the intellectual method to speaking and, once they understand how the various public speaking tools work, they will relish the opportunity to find their own tools that achieve the same purpose.

The immigrant population, irrespective of the country they come from or the country they have migrated to, will find this way valuable because it works at a deeper level than accents, language, and vocabulary. Immigrants often shy away from participating in discussions or delivering speeches because they do not speak the language of the locals or they speak the language with an accent. My approach to communications will clarify the role of accents, words, and language for the immigrant population. It will refocus their attention on the most important aspect of communication, the transfer of emotions, and provide them with the hope and confidence that they too can deliver effective speeches in front of an audience.

Finally, here's a word of caution. You have immense power to influence people. Your words can make people cry or they can make them laugh. You have the power to motivate, encourage, and inspire with the words you say. You can change lives through your speeches. As you develop as an effective communicator, you will feel this power and it is addictive. Great communicators learn to use this power for the greater good. I hope this book helps you realize this power and the responsibility that comes with it.

Good luck. Let the journey begin.

The Proposition

If you could deliver a speech that people will remember for
the rest of their lives—how powerful is that thought?
—Vikas Jhingran

I remember it like it was yesterday. I first heard about it on National Public Radio during my drive to work. The newscaster said, in only a few words, that a plane had collided into one of the World Trade Center towers. The size of the plane or the damage caused was not mentioned, giving no indication of the magnitude of the calamity that unfolded later in the day. I remember walking into my office building to find a group of people discussing this event. A few minutes later, a colleague shared some new information: another plane had collided into the second World Trade Center tower. I remember not being able to concentrate all morning, going from one Website to another to get more information. I remember it like it was yesterday.

I remember on my way home that evening, being stopped by a high school student who uttered racial slurs from the window of his pickup truck because he thought I looked like someone who would fly planes into buildings. I remember our conversation almost getting to the point of physical blows, the two of us standing at a U-turn median, our cars blocking the median in rush-hour Houston traffic. I remember it like it was yesterday.

I remember approaching a police officer later that evening and requesting him to be extra careful because of racial tensions. I remember it like it was yesterday.

It is difficult to imagine that this incident took place a decade ago, particularly because I remember some aspects of it so clearly. My wife finds this very surprising, especially because I have a hard time recalling the shopping list she gave me yesterday. I am not alone in having such graphic memories of September 11, 2001. In my workshops on public speaking, I often describe how vividly I remember the events that occurred that day, and my audience usually has similarly detailed memories. They too recall specific details, where they were when they heard the news the first time, what they were they wearing, and who told them the news. It is truly incredible.

I have often wondered, what makes 9/11 so memorable? Was it the shock of the event? Was it the image of the towers falling to the ground? Was it the loss of so many lives? Why do so many people remember that day? As a speaker, understanding how an event can become so memorable is important to me. Is there something in 9/11 that can help me understand the psychology of people, about how we process and remember things, that will let me deliver a speech that is so memorable that people will walk up to me 10 years later and say, "I was in the audience that day and I remember it like it was yesterday"?

I know this is possible because I have delivered speeches that people still remember many years later. This book is written to help you deliver your memorable speech—something that your audience will remember for the rest of their lives.

Part I

The Fundamentals

Chapter 1

The Importance of Effective Verbal Communication

When you talk, you give yourself away. You reveal your true character in a picture which is more true and realistic than anything an artist can do.
—Dr. Ralph Smedley, founder, Toastmasters International

"Every once in a while, a revolutionary product comes along that changes everything." So began the late Steve Jobs as he introduced the iPhone at the Macworld Expo in January 2007. Wearing his trademark black turtleneck and washed-out blue jeans, Jobs went on to deliver another amazing keynote speech. The energized audience punctuated his keynote with applause, knowing that they were witnessing the introduction of yet another revolutionary Apple product.

"In a career of dazzling product presentations, this [the iPhone launch] may have been his best," writes Walter Isaacson in his biography of Steve Jobs. Many agree with Isaacson, calling Jobs's 2007 Macworld Pro speech one of the greatest product launch presentations of all time. Like other presentations by Jobs, known as Stevenotes, the iPhone launch presentation was exquisitely planned and executed, resulting in unprecedented product hype and unparalleled advertising. His presentation slides were simple, conveying key ideas that created excitement in the audience. As in his other launch presentations, he did a live demonstration of the iPhone on stage, exuding the enthusiasm that he expected to see in his customers. Simply put, Steve Jobs enhanced the value of the iPhone through his product launch presentation. Today, in spite of immense competition and razor-thin profit margins in the consumer electronics sector, Apple products command a premium like no other electronic gadget manufacturer. At least part of the credit goes to the excellent communications strategy of Steve Jobs and his team.

The ability to communicate effectively is becoming an important differentiator in the corporate environment, particularly since corporations like Apple are going to all parts of the world in search of talent and lower costs. Our global, interconnected world requires people to communicate effectively in spite of differing backgrounds, cultures, and languages. Recent research published in January 2012 on the *Harvard Business Review* blog shows strong communication skills to be one of the nine traits exhibited by successful global leaders. Corporate recruiters consistently highlight the importance of communication skills in candidates.

In an online Harris Interactive survey of the 4,125 MBA recruiters, the results of which were reported in the September 20, 2006 issue of the *Wall Street Journal*, 89 percent identified interpersonal and communication skills as an important leadership trait that they seek in good candidates. The ability of corporate management to verbalize company goals and visions in diverse settings, something that the late Steve Jobs did so effectively for Apple, will be a key determining factor between companies that succeed and those that do not.

Despite this, I am amazed how little time and effort are invested by corporations in helping employees become effective communicators. Elaborate training programs exist to enable technical growth and business leadership development, but few programs, if any, target the oratory skills of employees. The training programs that are communication-focused typically teach a few tricks or tools to make messages stick. Employees do not develop a deeper understanding of verbal communication. There is no permanent learning.

|||||||||||||||||||||||||||||||||||||||||||||||||||||||||||||||||||||||||||||||||||||||||||

Importance of Communication:
A Business Example

Some time ago, I had the opportunity to manage the fabrication of some large structures for a schedule-driven project. Previous experience on similar projects had shown that the schedule I was being asked to meet was at best "aggressive" and most likely "improbable." To make matters worse, there was a large commercial consequence for delayed completion.

Very early in the project, I determined that the fabricator could meet schedule if I effectively managed communication to and from the fabricator. There were many stakeholders, each with valid concerns. The tight schedule and enormous consequences of failure ensured that I would have their full attention throughout the project. It became evident to me that to meet the deadline, I would have to manage the stakeholders so that they let the fabricators do their job. If the stakeholders communicated directly with the fabricator, it would lead to confusion and relationship disagreements with direct impact on the schedule.

I therefore posed the following question: if I am a stakeholder on this project, how should I feel during the fabrication process to not have the urge to communicate directly with the fabricator? I determined that:

a. If the stakeholders feel that the fabrication is on schedule and under control, they will not have the urge to communicate frequently with the fabricator.

b. If the stakeholders do need to communicate with the fabricator, they will likely follow a communication protocol if a clear communication protocol exists.

Thus, I established a clear communication protocol for the fabrication team. The stakeholders were not to talk directly with the fabricator, but only through me. On the fabricator's side, communication was to only go through their project manager. This allowed for an hourglass approach to communications, where all communication from the stakeholders was funneled through me to the project manager for the fabricator, who then distributed the communication to the appropriate people on the fabricator's team. The project manager and I could sift through the issues that the stakeholders had brought up and only communicate the necessary issues to the fabrication team. This approach greatly reduced confusion and increased focus and productivity.

Second, I established a process of continually updating the stakeholders on the progress of the fabrication. This included providing them with a status update, highlighting key achievements, arranging site visits, and addressing potential challenges ahead of time. In addition, pictures of the fabrication work and key milestones were sent to the stakeholders in a timely manner. These efforts kept the stakeholders from going into a crisis mode and the fabricators were left alone to finish their work. The project was finished on schedule.

The project was technical in nature, but the key reason for success was a good communication strategy.

||||||||||||||||||||||||||||||||||||||||||||||||||||||||||||||||||||||||||||||||||||||||||||||

Recently, I attended a four-day workshop on influencing corporate decisions. The attendees came from all parts of the world and, though not by design, represented many different personality types. I also noticed that the participants, both male and female, had different levels of comfort in verbal communication. One full day of this dynamic and high-energy workshop was dedicated to communication strategies, with an emphasis on verbal communication. Though the material on communication strategies was useful (it provided a list of tricks), it did not build a deeper understanding of communication. The workshop did not discuss how different personality types would use each communication tool or even discuss the idea that certain tricks suited certain personalities and ethnic backgrounds. Every individual was given all the tools without the background information to understand which tool would be right for him or her.

The corporate bottom line is not the only area where verbal communication skills can make a difference for a company. Most companies provide mentoring avenues where experienced communicators can develop young and emerging talent by encouraging them and sharing ideas. Similarly, there are many occasions, such as retirement speeches, diversity events, successful project recognition celebrations, and safety-related discussions, where a few words, spoken in a coherent and eloquent manner, can positively influence the lives of coworkers.

Robert Patterson, a vice president at Shell Oil Company, understands the importance of personal stories in influencing behavior. Patterson has more than 600 people in his organization and is constantly seeking out colleagues with good work-associated stories—particularly relating to improving work safety—which can help personalize the behaviors he is encouraging in his group. In town hall meetings conducted every few months and attended by his entire team, he has colleagues share their stories before the entire group. This approach has proved effective in making concepts about work safety become personal and memorable.

Effective verbal communication is also critical in the social context. There is general agreement on the importance of effective communication within the household between spouses and between children and parents. Consider, also, the various opportunities you have to speak within your social circle: chatting at a gathering of friends, offering a toast at a wedding, and sometimes, unfortunately, eulogizing a loved one at a funeral. We are literally communicating with others every day of our lives.

||||||||||||||||||||||||||||||||||||||||||||||||||||||||||||||||||||||||||||||||||||||||||

The Retirement Speech

A few years ago, a manager (who was also one of my mentors) was retiring. This individual was liked and well respected, and his retirement celebration was attended by many of his colleagues. Interestingly, apart from his colleagues in management who were obligated to speak at the ceremony, I was one of only two others who stepped up to say a few words in his honor. My background in public speaking gave me courage to "roast" my mentor on his retirement. It was my way of thanking him for his time and efforts in helping my professional development. I am sure that there were many others who had a lot to say and many who wanted to thank him for his friendship and guidance. They just did not have the courage to stand up in front of the large crowd and say a few words. They likely expressed their appreciation and gratitude to him in a one-on-one conversation or by e-mail.

||||||||||||||||||||||||||||||||||||||||||||||||||||||||||||||||||||||||||||||||||||||||||

Today's technology has further broadened our communication reach, enabling us to be connected to people in ways that were not possible even a decade ago. Social media Websites like LinkedIn and Facebook allow us to be "friends" with hundreds of people all over the world, many of whom we have never met or talked to in person. Add to that the ability to upload video and audio files on these and other Websites like YouTube, and it is now possible for speeches and talks to be shared with complete strangers, increasing our verbal communication footprint to cover the entire world. Few of us, however, realize that using videos and audio files to influence our Facebook "friends," with their varied backgrounds and sensitivities, requires great skill and a deep understanding of the fundamentals of verbal communication.

The late Randy Pausch, a former professor at Carnegie Mellon University, experienced the power of this influence when he became an overnight worldwide phenomenon. In 2007, Randy was asked to participate in a speaking series called the "The Last Lecture." The premise of such a lecture is interesting. It invites speakers to deliver a life-changing speech while assuming that this is their last speech on earth. The organizers hope that this role play will require speakers to introspect and share their life lessons with their audience. In the case of Randy Pausch, the scenario of impending death was not fictitious. Randy had been diagnosed with pancreatic cancer. The day that he sent the title of his speech to the event organizers was also the day he found out that his treatment had not worked.

He had a few months to live.

Pausch's lecture, called "Really Achieving Your Childhood Dreams," was delivered in a packed auditorium to an audience of 400 students and professors. Randy gave an emotional presentation, but the most telling moment of the speech came right at the end. On the last slide, Randy told his audience that the real purpose of his talk that day was not to motivate them but to leave a permanent recording for his three children who will grow up without him. This was his way of telling them how to live their lives, his way of imparting life lessons to his children. It was a beautiful speech that made a difference in the lives of everyone in the audience.

The amazing thing, which even Pausch did not comprehend at the time, was that the impact was not limited to his audience and his children. Versions of the recorded speech were posted on YouTube and became viral. The speech was seen by more than six million people, and affected them in a positive way. The popularity of the speech led Randy to write a book, appropriately called *The Last Lecture*. He was invited on various television talk shows. ABC Network named him the person of the year in 2007 and broadcast an hour-long segment on his life. "The Last Lecture" became one of the most watched videos on the Internet in 2007. More than 10 million copies of the lecture have been downloaded to date and more than five million copies of his book have been sold. Though Pausch died in July 2008, he left his wife and children a legacy of hope and inspiration. One speech made that happen.

There are also many indirect benefits of good communication. As you read this book, it will become clear that effective communicators have a strong understanding of emotions. They engage people at a much deeper degree than words or slides; they engage them at an emotional level. Thus, the process of developing effective communication skills leads to a deep understanding of emotions, creating the ability to work with your own emotions and those of others. This ability to work with and understand emotions is called emotional intelligence or EI, a concept made popular by Daniel Goleman in his 1994 best-seller, *Emotional Intelligence*. Since then, the benefits of high EI have been studied extensively in both business and social environments, and the results are eye-opening. Many of these studies, for example, have shown a strong correlation between a high emotional quotient and success in a corporate environment, indicating good corporate leaders are, among other things, emotionally intelligent people.

The approach to public speaking discussed in this book is particularly suited to develop emotional intelligence in people, leading to benefits far beyond the realm of communications. The ability to understand and convey emotions is the core of this speaking approach and Chapter 13 explores its ramifications in detail.

Effective speakers also relish the opportunity to evaluate situations and provide feedback. Research has indicated that people, both in corporate and social settings, struggle to provide difficult but essential feedback. This could be from something as simple as giving pointers to a child to improve on a recent dance performance to conducting an effective "lessons learned" exercise after a big project to communicating ways of improving vendor performance. Typically, feedback that does not consider the emotional implications for the person receiving it is bound to produce unintended consequences.

Many years ago, I gave some feedback to a speaker who obviously needed a lot of help in the area of public speaking. My critique was in front of a group of about 20 people. I did not shy away from pointing out the areas where the speaker needed to improve, and there were many. At the end of my feedback session, it seemed like I had been very critical, simply because there were many more things that the speaker did wrong than right. The speaker was so mortified by my feedback, however, that he never came back to the forum again. Though my intentions were good, I did not consider the emotional impact of my criticism on the speaker and ended up doing more harm than good. This ability to evaluate situations and provide effective feedback is the hallmark of a good listener.

Leaders who are good listeners develop the ability to "listen to" situations and provide feedback while keeping emotions in mind. In a corporate setting, this ability to listen comes in handy during team dynamics, mentoring opportunities, and problem solving. The impact of this speaking approach on developing listening skills is explored in Chapter 14.

Most verbal communication, even a speech, is not a monologue but a dialogue. In a speech, even though the words and ideas are going only from speaker to audience, there is always a back and forth of emotions. Good verbal communicators are able to evaluate the emotions of their audience and convey the necessary emotions back to them using tools like words, gestures, and voice modulation. These are difficult skills to develop, but the benefits make the effort well worth it. The next few chapters will provide you with the background and understanding to develop these skills and propel you toward becoming a more effective communicator.

How to Read This Book

This book, written with an emphasis on speaking in public, outlines a novel way to verbal communication. Though the basis is public speaking, the method can easily be applied to other forms of verbal communication. Whether it is a one-on-one talk with a senior manager, a group discussion with colleagues, or a town hall meeting with your team, this approach will help in all these communication formats.

The heart of the approach is discussed in Section I, called "The Fundamentals." Though the speech will be the communication format chosen to explain this technique, feel free to reflect on how these ideas may apply to your preferred method of verbal communication. As the ideas are discussed, consider situations in your daily life—professional or social—where you can use these ideas to increase your effectiveness as a communicator.

Section II discusses some tools that allow for the successful implementation of ideas discussed in Section I. Again, the tools discussed are in terms of speeches, but take the time to reflect on how these tools apply to your communication format, whether it is a small table discussion or a workshop-style event. In many cases, I explain how the use of these tools is different in the various verbal communication formats. For example, the use of a story is discussed as a tool in delivering effective speeches. However, stories are useful to make points in social settings as well. Have you noticed that the best conversationalist in a party is also the best storyteller?

An important aspect of this approach is that the foundation of verbal communication is essentially the same through all verbal communication formats, but the tools are either different or used differently within these various formats. It is common to find people who excel in one format of verbal communication, like the one-on-one, but are miserable in another, like speaking in front of a large group. I contend that one of the reasons for this apparent contradiction is that they are using the same speaking tools for both communication formats. There will be more on this interesting idea in Section II.

Section II also discusses two important topics: the impact of personality types on the choice of tools, and how ethnic and cultural backgrounds influence the choice of speaking tools. Introverts and extraverts, who have very different personality traits, will likely choose different speaking tools to achieve the same purpose. Similarly, speakers from Asia and the Middle East may have cultural reasons to avoid making eye contact, a commonly used speaking tool, and thus may prefer a different tool to achieve the same purpose.

Finally, Section III discusses the many indirect benefits of developing effective speaking skills. This section examines the role of this speaking approach in enhancing emotional intelligence and how good listening skills form the foundation of effective verbal communication.

The book is primarily about verbal communication and does not address other forms of communication—in particular, written communication skills that are used in books, blogs, e-mail, and texting. Though some aspects of my method do apply to these forms of communication, the difference in the medium causes some significant deviations. As an example, written communication is, by its nature, not "in the moment." The emotions of the writer have to be understood by the reader using the written word. In this situation, words carry a lot more importance than in speaking. For the same reason, recorded speeches, though addressed in this book, are also different. The audience is not present when the speech is delivered and has to gauge the emotions based on the video. The audience in a recorded speech also has the ability to go back and listen to each word again and again, thereby making the right choice of words far more important than in a live speech.

Chapter 2

What Is a Speech?

Successful people ask better questions, and as a result,
they get better answers.
—Anthony Robbins

After finishing my master of science degree in 1997, I found employment in the oil and gas sector in the city of Houston, Texas. Though I was doing well, my search for continued improvement led me, in 2004, to accept an opportunity to pursue a PhD at the Massachusetts Institute of Technology. MIT, as the institute is popularly called, is located near the city of Boston in the Northeastern state of Massachusetts.

For someone moving from the heat of Texas, the change was quite difficult. My wife and I were used to the subtropical climate in Houston and had never lived in a city like Boston, with a cold climate where winter snow is common. I remember the first winter in Boston when we had 36 inches of snow over a weekend in November. After the storm, I came out to find my car completely covered. Not knowing better, I started to remove the snow using my bare hands. My neighbor, who probably could not believe what he was seeing, came over and told me about the various tools I would need to survive a Boston winter. During the next few days, we made multiple trips to local stores to "winterize" ourselves with scrapers, shovels, thermal linings, and other winter gear.

But the weather wasn't my only adjustment. I had been out of a university environment for eight years and going back was not easy. My thesis advisor, Dr. Kim Vandiver, was a renowned researcher and also the dean of undergraduate research at MIT. In other words, time was an important commodity for him.

My first semester was exciting but amazingly busy. My research team had a big experiment to perform and I had to pass my PhD qualifying exams in addition to the usual course work. From the second semester onward, I started work on my thesis. I soon noticed that Dr. Vandiver almost never remembered my actual thesis work. He would repeatedly ask me what I was doing and how I was approaching my thesis problem. I assumed that he was busy with so many things that he just forgot what I was doing. In order to address this issue, I started my weekly meetings by reminding him of my thesis topic, restating how I planned to solve the problem and then finally showing him the progress for that week. This went on for many months. I found the state of affairs a little disconcerting; guiding a student through the process of getting a doctorate degree is difficult if you can't remember the topic your student is working on!

Months later it became apparent what Dr. Vandiver had been trying to do. There is a big difference between stating the problem and understanding the problem. In trying to explain time and time again to Dr. Vandiver what I was doing, I finally understood what I was doing. Dr. Vandiver had known all along that if I did not deeply understand and appreciate the engineering problem I was working on, I had little hope of trying to solve it. It was a very effective and interesting approach, and a lesson that I will never forget.

Dr. Vandiver's approach is the basis for this chapter, because our journeys as speakers can only begin after we understand the problems we are trying to address. I am sure that you have been exposed to many oral presentations in your lifetime. In middle and high school, you may have been asked to prepare and deliver presentations on year-end projects. In college, you may have participated in group discussions and made presentations with PowerPoint and other multimedia tools. Maybe you made or attended presentations as part of your undergraduate, graduate, or doctoral thesis requirements. If you work in corporate America, you've likely come across many presentations, weekly meeting reports, project updates, leadership town hall meetings, or safety update reports. In short, presentations and speeches are an integral part of our lives. That is why the question I am about to ask you may be strange.

Do you know what a speech is?

This question is not trivial because, let's be honest, an overwhelming majority of us have never defined a speech for ourselves. Remember the last time you were asked to deliver a speech. Did you think about what you were trying to do, or did you just gather the information, prepare the slides, and deliver the presentation? If you did the latter, you are not alone. Most people, when asked to report on something, do exactly that. They put forward the numbers and the logic that enabled them to reach a particular conclusion. If a project update is required, usually the presentations contain metrics, like projected costs vs. actual costs, projected schedule vs. actual schedule, updates on the project safety indicators, and so on. But this information can also be conveyed in a report, so why is a presentation necessary?

One of the first things I do in my workshops on public speaking is to ask my audience the question, "What is a speech?" I have found that this question is so simple and fundamental that it stumps most attendees. They begin immediately to answer it but then fumble for words and a definition for something that they think is obvious. This usually leads to interesting conversations around definitions of communication and a speech. Typically, this results in a keen awareness on the part of the workshop participants that their progress as speakers will be greatly enhanced if they put some thought into answering this question. In my experience, this is one of the main reasons keeping people from writing and delivering good speeches and presentations. As strange as it may sound, people just don't know what they are supposed to do when they get up and speak.

Let's Learn From History

In many of the old civilizations, early history was communicated in the form of oral stories passed down from one generation to the next. In the Indian subcontinent, the great mythological epics, called Itihasas, were told as stories by parents and grandparents to children for generations before they were written down many centuries later. It is interesting how these epics try to convey subtle messages using elaborate stories, showing us that the power of stories to enhance memory and generate interest was understood even in 2000 BC.

In the epic *Mahabharata*, a notable debate occurs between the learned King Janaka and an ascetic woman named Sulabha in which Sulabha emphasizes the essential skill of a good speaker:

> When, in the matter of what is to be said, the speaker shows disregard for the understanding of the hearer by uttering words whose meaning is understood by himself, then, however good those words may be, they become incapable of being seized by the hearer.
>
> That speaker, however, who employs words that are, while expressing his own meaning, intelligible to the hearer, as well, truly deserves to be called a speaker.

Isn't it noteworthy that Sulabha judges a speaker not by eloquence but how well the message is communicated to the listener? Perhaps our fascination with the eloquence of a speaker is misplaced.

The emergence of written history around 500 BC records the thoughts of leaders and orators from that era for review by modern historians. The ideas put forth by intellectuals and historians provide a fascinating discourse on what makes great communicators. Considered in context, whether it be leading an army to war or minimizing social unrest, they provide unparalleled access to wisdom and knowledge gained over centuries. It would be foolish for a speaker not to tap into this wealth of knowledge.

Consider the first references that emphasize the importance of communication, which are, not surprisingly, related to leading armies to war. In the ancient Chinese text *The Art of War*, Sun Tzu (500 BC) says, "If words of command are not clear and distinct, if orders are not thoroughly understood, the general is to blame." Though the context was war, Sun Tzu's words echo the ideas voiced by Sulabha that a good communicator makes sure that his or her message is understood. Both Sun Tzu and Sulabha emphasize the importance of conveying the message rather than the eloquence of the orator.

The work on rhetoric by Greek philosophers around 400 BC also provides deep insight on various aspects of verbal communication. Socrates (469–399 BC), for example, writes the following about rhetoric: "Is not rhetoric, taken generally, a universal art of enchanting the mind by arguments;

which is practiced not only in courts and public assemblies, but in private houses also, having to do with all matters, great as well as small, good and bad alike, and is in all equally right, and equally to be esteemed" (Williams, 210). Socrates emphasized, among other things, that rhetoric required the speaker to understand the "soul" of his audience as well as his speech. It introduces the concept, which we will discuss later, that a good speaker puts himself into the shoes of his audience to understand the effect of his words.

Aristotle, who lived two generations after Socrates, developed the most comprehensive treatise of rhetoric and the precursor to the modern term, public speaking. Among many amazing insights, Aristotle offers the following on rhetoric: "[It is the] faculty of discovering in any particular case all of the available means of persuasion." Note that the primary context during his time was avoiding social unrest among citizens and his "available means of persuasion" were developed in that context (Hartelius, 34). Aristotle's famous contribution was to define persuasion to be a result of three things: a) the genuineness of the speaker (ethos), b) the emotions aroused by the speaker (pathos), and c) the reasoning of the speaker (logos).

Socrates and Aristotle contributed tremendously to our understanding of verbal communication. Their philosophy of rhetoric emphasized the end effects or the result of communication and not the tools that were used to achieve that effect. In fact, one gets the sense that Aristotle will use whatever tools necessary to persuade his audience. This de-coupling of the mechanics of verbal communication and the results of communication is an important lesson for modern communicators.

The Roman orators and philosophers echo some of the wisdom of Aristotle and Socrates. Consider the works of Cicero, a Roman philosopher who was also a great orator. He, like Aristotle, regarded rhetoric as a "speech designed to persuade" (Howard, 171). Think, as well, of Quintilian, a Spanish philosopher who followed Cicero, who considered rhetoric as "the art of speaking well" (Howard, 171). Quintilian also provided structure to the speech preparation process by organizing the practice of oratory into five canons: inventio (discovery of arguments), dispositio (arrangement of arguments), elocutio (expression or style), memoria (memorization), and pronuntiatio (delivery).

Are these old ideas relevant to the modern world of communication? Can ideas discussed thousands of years ago be effective for communicators today? The answer is yes and it highlights a critical concept that few communicators understand. It shows that verbal communication at a fundamental level has not changed over centuries; only the tools used by speakers have changed. This remarkable fact lets us use insights gained two millennia ago in communication today.

How can I be so confident that these ancient ideas still work? One way is to compare them with what philosophers and communicators are saying about rhetoric today. Consider the thoughts put forth by George Campbell (1719–1796), a Scottish philosopher and professor, who says that rhetoric is "that art or talent by which discourse is adapted to its end. The four ends of discourse are to enlighten the understanding, please the imagination, move the passion, and influence the will" (Howard, 172). Campbell's view of rhetoric bears similarities with Aristotle's view that the aim of rhetoric is to persuade by any means available. Campbell, like Aristotle, is focused on the ends and not the means. A good perspective on effective speaking is given by Swami Vivekananda (1863–1902), an Indian philosopher who gained recognition in the Western world for his dynamic speeches but was not a scholar of rhetoric. In one of his essays he writes:

> Then again, when they speak, the world is bound to listen. When they speak, each word is direct; it bursts like a bomb-shell. What is in the word, unless it has the power behind? What matters it what language you speak, and how you arrange your language? What matters it whether you speak correct grammar or with fine rhetoric? What matters it whether your language is ornamental or not? The question is whether or not you have anything to give. It is a question of giving and taking, and not listening. Have you anything to give?—that is the first question. If you have, then give. Words but convey the gift: it is but one of the many modes.

Vivekananda offers great wisdom by saying that grammar, pronunciation, and word arrangements do not make for a great communicator. This realization is the mark of a speaker who understands that a speech is not to be confused with the tools used to deliver it. Kenneth Burke (1897–1993), a famous American literary theorist, also emphasizes the end result of a speech rather than the tools when he says "the basic function of rhetoric [is] the use of words by human agents to form attitudes or to induce actions in other human agents" (Howard, 172). Burke and Vivekananda are emphasizing, in their own way, the concepts that Sulabha, Sun Tzu, Aristotle, and Cicero had reinforced: that the meaning has to be conveyed, and the communication tools are not important. Good communicators in the modern era are aligned with their ancient counterparts: that verbal communication is much deeper than words and gestures. At a fundamental level, verbal communication is independent of language, culture, and background.

Well then, what is a speech? An interesting and fundamental outlook of verbal communication, one that encompasses many of the ideas proposed so far, is captured by George A. Kennedy, professor of rhetoric and author of *A Hoot in the Dark* (1992). He says: "Rhetoric in the most general sense may perhaps be identified with the energy inherent in communication: the emotional energy that impels the speaker to speak, the physical energy expanded in the utterance, the energy level coded in the message, and the energy experienced by the recipient in decoding the message." This idea of flow of energy as a way to understand communication is enlightening. It approaches communication at a fundamental level, yet is consistent with other observations that separate the speech from the tools used to deliver it.

Unlike these great philosophers and orators, you don't have a lifetime to devote to the subject of public speaking. However, some thought on the topic will help define your approach to speaking. This will help crystallize the discussions that follow, making the exercises and stories in this book both clear and practical. This underlying understanding of a speech will form the foundation on which all other aspects of speaking can be built. It is this understanding that you have to develop in this chapter.

My Definition of a Speech

In 2007, the year I won the World Championship of Public Speaking, I developed a definition of a speech. I defined it as an "emotional roller-coaster ride for the speaker and his audience." My definition was based on my environment at that time—speech competitions, where I had to make a strong impact on an audience in just seven minutes. I found that this could only be done by working with emotions, both mine and of the audience. I discovered that speeches could be made memorable by using a unique approach of identifying the right emotions, then writing and delivering a speech that generates those emotions in the audience. A speech for me became the emotional journey and distinctly different from how it was achieved. If it required that I say no words, I would do that because the emotions were what I was trying to convey. Implicit in this definition was that I knew where the journey would finish, which meant that the speech had good content and a clearly defined message or purpose. This message helped me identify the final emotion of the speech, a process I describe later in this book. I felt that if I could successfully convey this final emotion to the audience, I would have delivered a good speech.

The result, among other speeches, was "The Swami's Question," a seven-minute story of my struggle to excel in academics and my eventual acceptance to MIT for graduate studies. I used this speech in the finals of the World Championship in front of a 2,000-strong audience. The speech had a range of emotions. It used a variety of tools to convey those emotions and it left the audience with a deep, profound final emotion. All the audience members I talked to afterward said they had gone on an emotional journey with me and the speech, particularly at the end, had made a strong emotional impact. I had succeeded in conveying the emotion I had in mind. It also turned out to be good enough to win the World Championship.

I have stayed with this approach to speaking because it works, with minor adjustments, for most of the speaking situations I have encountered. There are two important components that make a speech successful using this method. The first is understanding the emotions that need to be conveyed. I realized that the only way to take an audience on an emotional journey was by going on the journey myself. It helped to talk from personal experience, though that is not a requirement. In my speeches, I "live" the emotions I am trying to convey. This in itself is a very powerful concept. How many times have you teared up because someone near you was in tears? How many times have you rolled in laughter because the person beside you could not stop laughing? Emotions are contagious, and if the speaker gets emotional, so will his or her audience.

‖‖‖

Communication Is an Emotional Experience

The concept that communication is an emotional experience has been discussed by others in recent years. Seth Godin, a marketing guru, once was so distraught about sitting through poor PowerPoint presentations that he wrote a short e-book on how to make good PowerPoint presentations. In this book he writes:

Communication is the transfer of emotion.

Communication is about getting others to adopt your point of view, to help them understand why you're excited (or sad, or optimistic or whatever else you are). If all you want to do is create a file of facts and figures, then cancel the meeting and send in a report.

Our brains have two sides. The right side is emotional, musical, and moody. The left side is focused on dexterity, facts, and hard data. When you show up to give a presentation, people want to use both parts of their brain. So they use the right side to judge the way you talk, the way you dress, and your body language. Often, people come to a conclusion about your presentation by the time you're on the second slide. After that, it's often too late for your bullet points to do you much good.

You can wreck a communication process with lousy logic or unsupported facts, but you can't complete it without emotion. Logic is not enough.

‖‖‖

The second component of the speech is the ability to take my audience on the emotional journey with me. This is different from getting the audience emotional during certain parts of the speech. The audience members have to feel that they lived the speech and the emotions that they felt were theirs. This is where mastering the mechanics of speaking is useful. I use some of the tools at my disposal to first connect with the audience, and then ensure that they stay connected and come along for the emotional journey.

I realized that at the end of a good speech, the audience will remember the emotions, particularly the final one that I leave them with. They will not remember the tools that I used to convey the emotions.

I do not, in any way, belittle the importance of having good facts, important information, and a clear message in a speech. Whereas those are the minimum requirements, they can also be conveyed to an audience as text. The identity of a good speech and other forms of verbal communication, their single most important characteristic, is this back and forth of emotion that can only happen when communication occurs in the moment. If that emotional exchange does not happen, then the soul of a speech is not realized. A speech then loses its distinguishing characteristic and ceases to be one. There are, of course, some other characteristics unique to speeches that include messages being communicated using multiple channels, including words, gestures, and pictures. In each case, as discussed in later sections of the book, the communication channels are most effective when they consider the emotions of the audience.

The Speech and the Mechanics of Speaking

Considerable confusion exists around the distinction between a speech and the mechanics of speaking. This confusion is seen even in some bestsellers like *Made to Stick* by Dan and Chip Heath. In their book, the authors identify six ways that will help people remember the key idea. The six ways are simplicity, unexpectedness, concreteness, credibility, emotions, and stories.

Though there are several interesting thoughts explored in this book, it highlights the lack of clarity that exists, even among the great thinkers in our society, around speeches and the mechanics of speaking. The truth is that at the end of a good speech, the audience only remembers how they feel. They do not remember the simplicity of the presentation, unexpectedness of the ideas, concreteness of the thoughts, or credibility of the speaker. All these are important tools that were used by the speaker to enhance the emotional experience of the audience. The speech is only the emotional experience and should not be grouped together with the tools. In fact, different speakers will use different proportions of the tools, as well as other tools not suggested by the authors, to deliver similar emotional experiences to their audience.

This lack of clarity leads to speakers trying to focus on the wrong things while speaking. A speaker, for example, may focus on trying to tell stories because he believes that it is a necessary part of a good speech. This speaker may try to do so even though he is a poor storyteller and is uncomfortable doing it. A good story certainly enhances the emotional experience of an audience but if the speaker is uncomfortable, the audience feels that discomfort and it greatly takes away from the emotional experience. The speaker would have been better off using a tool that he is comfortable with that produces the same emotional experience for the audience. I was once told by a member of the National Speakers Association that you have to use humor to be a paid speaker. Unfortunately, such statements confuse the distinction between the tools, in this case the use of humor in speeches, and the emotional experience of the audience. When a speaker who is uncomfortable using humor buys into this philosophy, she may be unable to provide the emotional experience for the audience because of discomfort with the use of this tool. She will do better choosing a tool that she is comfortable with and focusing on the emotional experience.

There are other disadvantages to focusing on the tools rather than the end result. Guidelines by most authors on the use of tools never provide clarity on how much of a tool to use. For example, many speakers extol the advantages of keeping a presentation simple. The obvious question is, how simple should my presentation be? Would one equation be too little in a technical presentation or are at least 10 equations required? Similarly, speakers that emphasize the importance of humor in speeches never reveal how much humor is needed. Is one humorous moment in a speech adequate or are multiple humorous moments required for an effective talk? Such lack of clarity, and many other similar examples, exists among the majority of speakers.

That being said, the tools can be very important in the hands of a speaker who understands the purpose of a speech and the limitations of tools, and is not afraid to switch to a more appropriate tool when the situation demands. A speaker with a clear understanding of the foundations will revel in the infinite opportunities that the speaking tools provide to work with emotions. He will understand when to use humor and why eye contact is effective. He will also understand the impact and clarity provided by effective stage use, the immense power of vocal variety, etc. When the foundations are clear, the possibilities for a speaker are truly endless.

Conclusions

So, did this chapter provide you with an "aha" moment—a realization that a speech is much deeper than you thought?

I also hope it provided you with a conviction that preparing a good speech is within your grasp because it requires you to share your emotions in an authentic way. It does not require you to be constrained by the mechanics of speaking but, rather, to use speaking tools as enablers of the transfer of emotion to your audience. This very realization opened the doors to tremendous growth in my speaking journey, and I hope it will have a similar effect on you.

You may also notice that this approach works for all modes of verbal communication, not just public speaking. The emphasis on emotions during a conversation is as effective in a one-on-one setting as it is before a thousand people. Effective communicators in one-on-one conversations understand that the words being spoken are only one way of receiving information. They actively look for more information from other tools like gestures, facial expressions, breathing patterns, speaking rates, and so on. They use this information collectively to form a picture of the emotional state of the person sitting across the table.

Interestingly, as Joe Navarro has often found, this emotional state may be contrary to what the person is saying. Navarro is a former FBI agent who, as part of his job, regularly used his knowledge of nonverbal communication to identify criminals. In his book, *What Every Body Is Saying*, he describes an arson incident and the role of the security guard in it. The security guard came under suspicion because the fire was in the area where he was assigned. During interrogation, Navarro noticed that the guard often squinted and blinked when asked about his whereabouts when the fire was started. Navarro knew that such eye-blocking behaviors were telltale signs of our brain avoiding undesirable images. The security guard, however, showed no eye-blocking behavior for all other questions, including, "Did you set the fire?" This led Navarro to correctly conclude that the security guard was lying about his whereabouts at the time of the fire. It turned out that an arsonist had set the fire while the security guard had left his post to visit his girlfriend.

By being aware of nonverbal signals, Navarro was able to understand the emotions of the security guard during their conversation, even though these emotions were contrary to what the guard was saying. This ability to read emotions conveyed by nonverbal signals is a quality found in many people who are good at face-to-face communication.

Now that we understand that speeches are, at their core, a back and forth of emotion, the next chapter discusses the second step to delivering memorable speeches: understanding human emotions. As humans, we are wired to emote, to understand, and to work with emotions. What we need to develop is a keener awareness of our emotions and an ability to communicate them using a speech. The communication of emotions can only follow the awareness and understanding of emotions. This is what we will discuss in Chapter 3.

Chapter 3

Working With Emotions

The best and most beautiful things in the world cannot be seen or even touched. They must be felt with the heart.

—Helen Keller

In 1994, while an undergraduate student at the Indian Institute of Technology, I took a class in the structural design of ships. The class was being taught by Dr. Madhujit Mukhopadhyay, a well-known professor in his field. That semester, I was also sending in applications to universities in the United States for graduate studies. I knew that a good recommendation from Dr. Mukhopadhyay would greatly increase my odds of an academic scholarship, and I was determined to impress him. Things had gone well until midway through the semester when a particular assignment was due. It turned out to be a busy week for me and I only got to the assignment the night before it was due. After struggling for a few hours, it was evident that this project was not a trivial exercise and I would not be able to finish it by the following morning. I knew that an extension was not possible, so I had two options: submit it late, forgo the grade, and look bad in the eyes of the professor, or seek help from a friend.

Though this was a "do it alone" assignment, I sought the help of a friend to finish it on time. The next morning, Murphy's Law took effect and an unlikely chain of events led to Dr. Mukhopadhyay finding out about my indiscretion. I still remember walking into class that day and seeing Dr. Mukhopadhyay's face dripping with disappointment. I remember his words: "Vikas, who are you fooling—me or yourself?"

His words, the embarrassment I felt, and fear of repercussions filled me with strong emotions. I was bitterly disappointed in letting Dr. Mukhopadhyay down. I was embarrassed that he, and all my classmates, had found out about my error in judgment. Finally, I feared repercussions, because the professor had considerable influence and was well known. In spite of the incident having occurred more than 15 years ago, I still remember it clearly. I remember the room in which it happened, where my professor was when he said those words, and how I felt at that time. I remember these details as if they were recorded in my brain and I could play the recording at will. I am sure you have had similar experiences in your life where you are able to recall an incident in detail many years after it occurred. Have you ever wondered why this is the case?

||||||||||||||||||||||||||||||||||||||||||||||||||||||||||||||||||||||||||||||||||||||||||||||

Can You Copyright Music?

Terry McBride, CEO of the Nettwerk Music Group, delivered an interesting speech at the 2009 TEDx conference in Vancouver. Terry suggested that music is an emotional experience for the audience. He then argued that this is a key reason for the ownership conflict between the music industry, which assumes that copyright equals ownership, and music listeners. Terry proposed that every music listener has a different emotional experience to the same piece of music. During this experience, listeners superimpose their thoughts and ideas on the emotions, making their experiences their own and rather unique. It is difficult for the listeners to understand how someone can "copyright" this unique experience that, in their minds, is theirs.

||||||||||||||||||||||||||||||||||||||||||||||||||||||||||||||||||||||||||||||||||||||||||||||

In the last few decades, extensive research on "emotional memory" has shown that strong emotions associated with an incident enhances the memory of that incident. In my personal story in the previous section, the strong emotions generated during the incident with the professor helped "peg" that memory. Molecular biologist John Medina in his book, *Brain Rules*, explains emotional memory: "When the brain detects an emotionally charged event, the Amygdala releases dopamine into the system. Because dopamine greatly aids memory and information processing, you could say it creates a 'Post-it' note that reads 'Remember this.'"

Apart from the memory-enhancing aspect, emotions also compel people to act. In the years following the incident with Dr. Mukhopadhyay, I developed a deep desire to be truthful to my core values. I realized that Dr. Mukhopadhyay had correctly pointed out that the only person I was fooling was me. I credit this incident as one of the reasons for my academic excellence in the following years. His question, "Who are you fooling?" continues to be a guiding light for me today. The impact of those words by Dr. Mukhopadhyay was profound because of the strong emotions they generated in me. They propelled me to take action.

The changes in the lives of people in the United States post-9/11 are a more dramatic example of emotions propelling action. Earlier in the book, I discussed how many people still have vivid memories of 9/11. Even though this is fascinating, equally incredible is the transformation that the United States has gone through as a result of September 11, 2001. A war in Afghanistan began immediately after, the war in Iraq followed. Internally, security systems at airports, along borders, and at ports have become much stricter at the cost of billions of dollars and in a very short time. The strong emotions of anger, fear, and contempt that were generated by the 9/11 tragedy were a key force behind all of these changes.

Though 9/11 is an extreme example, it is one that has left a profound emotional imprint on millions of people. They can see how their lives have changed as a direct consequence of those attacks. Those attacks are good examples of how emotions can propel a whole country—the politicians, the military, the people—to action.

Our daily lives are flush with examples of how emotions move us to act. Fear of a home burglary is the main reason for investing in a home security system, even though there may be no history of burglaries in the area. Anxiety over layoffs may result in personnel working harder than ever, though there may have been no basis for that anxiety. The evening news is chock-full of crime stories that were motivated by jealousy, greed, and anxiety. Big important actions, it seems, are particularly influenced by emotions.

This is where it becomes fascinating. We have just concluded that emotions—which enhance our memory of an incident, sometimes allowing us to remember it in graphic detail for many years—propel us to act, providing the necessary energy to enact large-scale or life-changing transformations in a relatively short time.

Wait! Aren't these the same things all of us are trying to do when we make presentations? Each one of us hates to be mundane. We want to be remembered long after our words are spoken. We also long to make a difference and move people toward a better life. If the results of using emotions in speeches are aligned with what we as presenters are aiming to do, can't we work with the emotions of the audience to make effective presentations? The answer is yes. If a speaker can learn the art of working with the emotions of an audience, he would be well on his way to delivering memorable speeches that will change lives. Our challenge is to develop a deeper understanding of emotion so that it is not a vague word used by psychologists, but a well-understood concept that speakers can use. This chapter helps develop this understanding.

‖‖

Emotions Help Us Remember

The idea of working with emotions to make messages memorable has been used by good musicians and movie directors for many years. Remember the final twist in the movie *The Sixth Sense* where the audience realizes for the first time that Dr. Malcolm Crowe, the lead character played by Bruce Willis, is already dead? The surprise was so strong that most people will remember it for years. I still remember the scene, the theatre where I saw the movie, and with whom I saw it. Similarly, musicians who are successful in getting their audience emotionally involved make pieces of music that stay with us for many years.

‖‖

What Are Emotions?

We all know what emotions are, don't we? After all, we feel them every day. You may feel joy early in the morning, then anxiety due to a delayed project when you get to work, anger at an inappropriate e-mail sent by a colleague, fear when your toddler's daycare informs you that he or she is having an asthma attack, and love later that evening when your whole family is together and your son or daughter is doing well. If these are just a few emotions in a typical day, imagine the range, both in number and intensity, of emotions that you will feel in your lifetime.

Our general understanding of emotions is captured well in definitions available in dictionaries and other non-scientific texts. For example, the online Oxford dictionary defines emotion as:

a. "A natural instinctive state of mind deriving from one's circumstances, mood, or relationships with others."

b. "Instinctive or intuitive feeling as distinguished from reasoning or knowledge."

This definition is in line with how most of us would define the word "emotion." We recognize that emotions define a state of mind and are due to external (relationships) and internal (moods) stimulus. We would clearly distinguish between cognitive and intellectual faculties and emotion, because our brains seem to be less "logical" when we are very emotional. Most of us also subscribe to the common idea that emotions are linked to the heart and logic is linked to the brain.

These simple definitions of emotion work for us in our daily lives but do not offer the depth of understanding that is required by an artist, be it a speaker, painter, or musician, who aims to influence his or her audience using emotions. We need to go deeper. However, as soon as we go a little deeper into understanding emotions, it reveals itself to be a very difficult problem. The immense complexity of this subject is reflected in the scientific definitions of emotion. Consider this: after centuries of living with emotions every day, there are still no "accepted" definitions of emotion. In fact, few psychologists tend to have a formal definition of emotion, saying that it is too complex a phenomenon to be captured in a few words.

Though the topic of emotions is incredibly complex, we do not have to become experts in the intricacies of emotion to be able to use them effectively in speeches. We do, however, have to understand, in greater detail, a few characteristics of emotions that are relevant to speaking.

Emotions Are Universal

Research has shown that people all over the world, irrespective of their upbringing and environment, feel similar emotions. The intensity (or valence) of these emotions may vary depending on the mood, environment, and past history, but most individuals will have emotionally similar reactions to events, particularly events that trigger strong emotions.

That emotions are relatively similar over the human species may be grounded in why they developed in the first place. At least some psychologists believe that emotions played an important role in the survival of our ancestors. Emotions such as fear allowed early man to run when danger was imminent, without even engaging the "thinking brain." Similarly, the emotion of anger propelled them to fight when they had been wronged by an intruder. The universality of emotions is on display at international sporting events like the Olympic Games. Hundreds of athletes from all over the world go through intense emotions during the games. Though these athletes speak different languages, come from various cultures, and have different religious beliefs and divergent life experiences, their reactions to the results of competition are remarkably similar. They all feel joy and elation in victory. They feel anguish and disappointment in defeat. They express frustration in injury and they all express immense pride in representing their countries.

This universality of emotional response is an important concept for a speaker. First, it allows a speaker to write speeches knowing that the same emotions that he feels can be aroused in his audience. For example, the speaker can rest assured that the sense of longing she feels when her children are away or the sense of anticipation before a delicious meal is shared by her fellow people all over the world. This seemingly obvious but truly remarkable feature of emotions provides speakers with a huge advantage in writing and delivering speeches. Second, the speaker can ask a small group of friends or mentors the question: "How do you feel when you hear this story?" The answer, in most cases, is a good representation of how the audience will feel anywhere in the world. The speaker can experiment with new techniques in front of a "friendly" audience, playing with speaking tools and changing stories, until the speech elicits the expected response from the "friendly" group. The speaker knows that the response from his intended audience will be similar. This is an unqualified asset in preparing and perfecting a speech.

II

Mirror Neurons

The scientific reason for why we become emotional by looking at others getting emotional may be explained by mirror neurons. Scientists have recently discovered an area in the brain that activates when watching others do activities and, perhaps more importantly for speakers, watching others get emotional. For example, fMRI scans show that the region of the brain related to emotion would light up when we feel a certain emotion but that area would also light up when we see someone else feel that emotion. The mirror neurons "feel" the emotions of others and then communicate them to the brain as if they are being felt by us.

Now you don't have to feel bad about getting teary eyed at the movies; you are wired to respond that way.

IIIIIIIIIIIIIIIIIIIIIIIIIIIIIIIIIIIIIIIIIIIIIIIIIIIIIIIIIIIIIIIIIIIIIIIIIIIIIIIIIIIIIIIIIIIIIIIIII

Not All Emotions Have Names

Have you ever had trouble finding the right word to explain your feelings? Emotions are so complex and varied that in many cases we struggle to name one that completely describes how we feel. Sometimes, the difficulty also has cultural and regional connotations. Many languages around the world have the same word for similar but different emotions. Different languages may also have many different words for similar emotions that distinguish between the nuances of an emotion. In his book, *What Is Emotion?*, Jerome Kagan writes about the language used by the Utku Inuit which has four different words for "loneliness." The distinctions are based on the source of the emotion; that is, why is someone feeling lonely? Similarly, the emotion arising from the complete acceptance of one by another person, called Amae, is unique to Japan (Fox, *Emotion Science*).

Due to this complexity, it is important that the speaker spends time understanding the emotions being evoked by her speech. For example, if the feeling aroused by a speech is "loneliness," the speaker should probe deeper and go beyond the initial answer of "I feel lonely." A speaker should continue to ask questions to understand the context of where the emotion comes from. In many instances, as a result of deeper probing, the speaker will find that the emotions evoked in the audience are not those he was trying to convey through his speech. This will lead the speaker to make adjustments to her speech, which may include choosing different stories or changing the flow of the speech.

Moods Are Different From Emotions

We commonly use the phrase "I'm not in the mood for...." It implies a general feeling lasting over an extended period of time. This is an accurate distinction from emotions, which generally occur over shorter periods of time. Psychologists believe that emotions take place over seconds, minutes, or hours, whereas moods may occur over hours, days, or months. Jesse Prinz, professor of philosophy at the City University of New York, distinguishes emotion from moods in his book *Gut Reactions: A Perceptual Theory of Emotion*. For Prinz, "moods are set up to detect global changes in organism-environment relations, while emotions are set up to detect localized changes."

For a speaker, this is an important distinction. It means that, though the speaker will be working with the emotions of an audience, their emotional response may be colored by the prevailing mood. It is impossible for a speaker to find out the mood of each person in the audience or, for that matter, write and deliver a speech that takes into account the mood of each audience member. However, a speaker should be aware of the global mood of the audience by researching recent events. His research may find, for example, that a loved community member recently passed away and the general mood of the crowd is gloomy and sad. Taking the background mood of the audience into account will help the speaker deliver the appropriate emotion. It will also help in identifying the initial emotion, a concept we will discuss in Chapter 4.

A gifted speaker or artist will understand the prevailing mood and emotion of the audience and meet them there. This allows the speaker to connect with them. Once the connection has been established, the speaker can then lead the audience on an emotional journey and end at a final emotion of her choice. An excellent example of this was brought to my attention after one of my speeches. At a conference in Washington, D.C., I had introduced the idea of a speaker meeting the audience at their emotional state to form a good connection. After my talk, an audience member came up to me and asked if I had seen the WWII Memorial. I had not. This gentleman then said:

> I can make a lot more sense of the memorial after hearing your speech. The memorial begins with a sense of chaos and war, with carnage and explosions everywhere but then slowly moves on and ends in a very calm and soothing place. I understand now that the memorial is trying to meet its audience at the prevailing mood or emotion, and slowly bring them to a better place, provide some calm and soothing to the audience.

He was right. The WWII Memorial is working with emotions without the spectators even realizing it.

I will be using the terms "feelings" and "emotions" interchangeably, though I understand that some researchers distinguish between them. For the purpose of this book, however, these differences are not important.

Emotion and Temperament

Different people react to emotions in different ways. An individual's response to emotional stimulus and his ability to control those emotions is called his temperament. People with different temperaments will offer different emotional responses to the same emotional stimuli. No wonder working with people is so difficult!

When speaking to large groups, the temperament of individuals is generally not important. A large sample will "average" out extreme emotional responses due to individual temperaments, enabling the speaker to work with the emotional response of the group rather than the individual. This response is much more predictable, allowing the speaker to, in most cases, make the same speech before multiple groups and receive similar emotional responses.

The influence of temperament on a one-on-one conversation is much greater. An equivalent scenario occurs in a presentation to a small group with one key decision-maker. The speaker, in these cases, has to be aware of the temperament of one person, setting up a feedback loop that allows for making adjustments to his presentation based on the response of this individual. Many of us make these adjustments without thought during a conversation. A skilled speaker in the presence of one person or a key decision-maker will go further and actively notice the temperament of this individual. The speaker may even devote the first few minutes of his presentation to investigating the temperament of this individual, engaging him in discussion or asking questions. A skilled speaker can then make changes to his presentation, emphasizing certain aspects or marginalizing other sections, based on his assessment of this individual's temperament.

Emotion and Personality Types

Different personalities are wired to process emotional stimuli differently. Consider the difference between introverts and extraverts. Research based on some seminal work done by Hans Eysenck shows that the reason extraverts are so social and outgoing is that their inherent levels of arousal, called cortical arousal, is low. Hence, to find the optimal level of arousal, they have to seek large external stimuli. Introverts, on the other hand, have a high cortical arousal and so prefer low levels of external stimuli to reach their optimal level of arousal. This fascinating research may throw light on how different personalities may respond to or absorb emotional stimuli.

Extraverts, based on this research, would revel in situations where the emotional levels are high around them. A typical example might be an extravert watching a football game in a stadium with thousands of shouting fans around her. The external emotional stimuli would supplement her inherently low cortical arousal levels, pushing her emotional experience into optimal levels of arousal. In short, she would really enjoy watching the game in the stadium setting. Other examples might be delivering a speech in front of a large enthusiastic crowd.

Introverts will distinguish themselves by being able to pick up very low levels of emotional signals, making them keenly aware of emotional changes occurring within them and around them. They will be able to read nonverbal signals much more quickly, because their intrinsically high cortical arousal levels allow them to sense small changes in emotional stimuli around them. In a typical situation, an introvert would become aware of negative emotions that have not been explicitly communicated in a conversation and would therefore be more likely to address them. Perhaps this is the reason why introverts are often regarded as better listeners; they just have a higher sensitivity in picking up small changes conveyed in emotions.

In his book, *Extraversion and Introversion,* author Larry Wayne Morris summarizes the difference in the way introverts and extraverts process emotion this way: "Thus the more extraverted person is emotionally inhibited but behaviorally expressive, whereas the more introverted person is behaviorally inhibited but experiences greater depth and variety of emotion."

The implications for speakers are enormous. An introverted speaker who understands that too much of the rush while speaking tires him out will minimize the time he spends in front of a high-octane, energy-exuding crowd, preferring discussion with a few people in a quieter setting after the speech. Similarly, an extraverted speaker who prepares a high-energy presentation for an introverted bunch of engineers should not be surprised when they are not jumping on their seats in applause during the speech. It also does not mean these engineers are not enjoying the presentation. An understanding of these differences in the emotional wiring between introverts and extraverts helps speakers tailor the emotional content of their speeches and the expectations of emotional responses to them.

Emotion and Cultures

People, in general, feel the same way and a speaker can take advantage of this fundamental concept to connect with audiences across all cultures and languages. My book is based on this very premise.

A distinction has to be drawn between felt emotion and the display of emotion. The first concept deals with what we feel. Many of the basic emotions have an evolutionary origin and were needed for survival. These emotions would be expected to remain the same across humanity, with thousands of years of evolution unlikely to be changed by a few hundred years of cultural differences. Do culture and environment, then, have no influence on felt emotions? There is research, by Phillip Shaver and his colleagues for example, that shows that some differences in felt emotions do exist across cultures. For example, the Chinese show a "sad love" emotion that is not common in America. This emotion covers feelings associated with infatuation, nostalgia, and sorrow/love. Americans understand these feelings but do not associate them with a basic emotion. It seems that there are many identified love-related feelings in Chinese culture that have sad connotations.

The display of emotions and the response to emotional stimuli may vary significantly between cultures. Cultural norms and social etiquette may significantly color the way people respond to emotions. A Japanese man, for example, who is uncomfortable in the presence of his superior may smile or laugh a lot. The response for a man in Western culture under similar emotional stimuli will likely be very different. Similarly, Western cultures that discourage the overt display of emotion during funerals differ from many other cultures where it is common, almost expected, to have the bereaved cry (sometimes hysterically) and display their grief in a very public way.

These differences in the response to emotional stimuli can be difficult to interpret and may lead to incorrect conclusions being felt by the responding individual. This is where their cultural influences on emotions may impact verbal communications that rely on nonverbal cues for much of the information exchange. Misinterpreted emotional cues can completely sidetrack a one-on-one discussion or lead to erroneous judgments on the appeal of a public speaker's message. An understanding of these cultural differences in emotional response can provide a speaker with a leg up, especially when speaking before an international audience.

The Basic Emotions

Have you ever thought how color printers are able to print all colors even though they only have blue, green, and red printer cartridges? Color printers utilize a concept in physics called the Theory of Primary Colors. This concept states that there are just three primary colors in the world—red, blue, and green. All colors that we see around us are just a combination of these three primary colors. This understanding of the physics of colors makes color printing possible. Many other parallels exist, especially in science and engineering.

Many psychologists believe a similar concept could explain emotions. They propose a few basic emotions—equivalent to the primary colors—that can be combined to explain all the emotional states we see around us. The simplicity of the idea has led many researchers to adopt this hypothesis. There is, however, considerable debate on what the basic emotions are. For the purposes of our discussion, let's consider the basic emotions suggested by Robert Plutchik. In his book, *Emotion: Theory, Research and Experience* (1980), Plutchik argues that the basic emotions are fear, anger, joy, sadness, trust, disgust, anticipation, and surprise. He identifies these as basic because, according to his research, all these emotions when triggered have high survival value for humankind. He therefore argues that these emotions must have existed in early humanity and played an important part in the survival of the human species. His thinking was that, as the human species evolved, all the other emotions came into being as a combination of the basic emotions.

The idea of basic emotions is a great way for a speaker to understand emotional states. All of us are generally aware of and understand the basic emotions, and can communicate them clearly. This, however, is not the case for other emotions that we feel on a daily basis. The basic emotions can help clarify how we are feeling for communication purposes.

Later in the book, you will realize why speakers have to understand the emotions they want to evoke in the audience. This understanding is the basis for a crucial concept in verbal communication, introduced in this book, called the final emotion. A skilled speaker can link the specific purpose of a speech to a feeling, understand the basic emotions that can cause the feeling, and then write a speech that generates these basic emotions. I will discuss this topic in detail in the next chapter.

As an exercise, consider any feeling you may have had in the past few days and try to break it down in terms of the basic emotions. For example, I remember being anxious in 2009 before a work-related presentation to a group of colleagues. The presentation was important and a good result could have hastened favorable consequences. However, I felt strongly that matters should not have come to this point and the presentation was only necessitated because of vocal criticism from a few uncooperative colleagues. The result was a high-stakes presentation where make-or-break decisions would be made.

I had all the trademark signs of anxiety: low attention span, muscular tension, difficulty sleeping, etc. There was certainly some anticipation. There was a feeling of fear that the presentation would not go well. I was also angry that the presentation was even necessary. Finally, I was a little distrustful of a few colleagues who had not cooperated with my effort. Hence, my anxiety was a mix of anticipation, fear, anger, and distrust.

Soft and Hard Emotions

The effect of each of the basic emotions is different. Emotions like joy, trust, and appreciation/love can be considered as softer emotions. These emotions have a soft impact on us—we can deal with them for hours and days without them having a "tiring" effect on us. Have you ever been to a stand-up comedy show? It's a lot of fun and, if the speakers are good, you could end up laughing continuously for the entire show. However, after a while, it begins to get tiring. According to Darren LaCroix, a stand-up comedian turned professional speaker, most stand-up comedy routines begin to lose their edge after 45 minutes to an hour. That's about how long it takes an average person to tire because of humor, which produces a soft emotion.

Other emotions like fear, anger, and surprise are harder emotions. The extreme form of these "hijacks" our brain, decapitating our cognitive ability as the emotions take control. The reason that emotions such as fear and anger are so strong might be traced to human survival instincts. These emotions have traditionally been associated with danger or war and activate large muscle regions, pumping them with blood for the required actions (flight or fight). The effects of these emotions are intense focus, strong overwhelming feelings, and fatigue if they continue for long. In their extreme form, these emotions bypass the cognitive brain and allow our muscles to act without "thinking."

These emotions can be potent if used appropriately but can also be all-consuming, leaving the audience tired and gasping for relief if used by an inexperienced speaker. Such examples of "emotional fatigue" are not as uncommon as you may believe. Consider the emotion of fear; sudden fear has a very strong impact on us. Our heart begins to pound and, in extreme cases, we are paralyzed, unable to act or think. A few minutes of this emotion will drain energy and tire you. This is why you don't have "stand-up fear shows": an average person wouldn't last for more than a few minutes.

A speaker must be aware of the concepts of basic emotions and soft and hard emotions to craft speeches that use them in the right quantities. Only then can the speaker have the desired impact. A speech that is half floor-rolling humor and half profound sadness will not produce equal amounts of joy and sadness in the audience. Sadness, being a stronger emotion, will overwhelm the speech.

‖‖

Other Theories That Explain Emotion

As with all things scientific, there exists another school of thought. A second theory suggests that all emotions are different and trying to explain them in terms of a few basic emotions trivializes their complexity. This theory suggests there are an infinite number of emotions that vary continuously along two axes, valence (good or bad emotion) and intensity (weak or strong emotion).

‖‖

Emotions and Memory

I still remember hearing the song "Sweet About Me" by Gabriella Cilmi for the first time on a flight back from Kuala Lumpur. I had just finished watching the movie *Revolutionary Road* on the flight entertainment system—a very memorable film because of how depressing it was. To change my mood, I decided to listen to the radio. The first song I played was "Sweet About Me." I am not an audiophile and hardly remember any song I hear but I remembered that song. Cilmi's song was a good one but the likely reason I remember it were the strong emotions I was experiencing that day after watching *Revolutionary Road*.

Traditionally, speakers are taught to enhance memory by repetition. This form of memory, sometimes also called "habit memory," is enhanced by repeating the same concept or act many times. This method of memorizing information is particularly common in technical presentations where speakers are, as Dale Carnegie puts it, encouraged to "tell the audience what you're going to say, say it; then tell them what you've said," with the implication that the repeated utterances of the same concepts (sometimes with different examples and ideas) will increase the likelihood that the audience will remember them. Workshop presenters use the same concept when they make participants practice a skill multiple times until they get it.

This "practice makes permanent" approach is not without merit and has been used successfully by many speakers and workshop presenters. However, it does require a lot of time for the skill or concept to become part of long-term memory.

A different approach to making messages memorable is by using emotions. In some interesting experiments by Elizabeth Kensinger and her colleagues at Boston College, subjects were shown pictures that were either emotionally neutral—chairs, tables, etc.—or emotionally charged, such as angry faces. The subjects tended to remember the pictures that had emotions in them better than the neutral images. This phenomenon is called emotional memory enhancement. More and more researchers think that a part of the brain called the amygdala is critical in enhancing memory of emotional events. Patients with damaged amygdalae did not show any enhancement of emotional images.

Functional magnetic resonance imaging (fMRI) allows researchers to "look" inside the brain and investigate which brain centers are being activated at a certain time. Some recent studies have used fMRI images of subjects to identify the role of the amygdala in making emotional memories. Kensinger and others now believe that the amygdala does not store emotional memories but enhances them by making sure they are noticed when the event occurs, creating a better cataloguing system so that they can be retrieved. In other words, emotions with the help of the amygdala trigger a better filing system for memories.

Nowhere has the emotional enhancement of memory been more widely used than in business schools. Many years ago, Harvard adopted a case study approach to learning in business schools. This approach used a story, where different characters were given personalities and a history, and the students were asked to put themselves in the shoes of the characters. This allowed them to get emotionally connected to the beliefs and thought processes of the characters. What usually follows are passionate discussions, filled with emotional content that makes the discussions and the following "debrief" by the professor memorable. This method has been so successful that it is difficult to find an MBA program in the world where case studies are not used to teach students.

Flashbulb Memories

The date was January 28, 1986. The city of Concord, New Hampshire was beaming with excitement. Their own Christa McAuliffe was going to be on a shuttle blasting off into space. The year before, Christa had been selected from more than 11,000 applicants to be the first astronaut in space as part of the NASA Teacher in Space Project. Though her family was from Framingham, Massachusetts, Christa taught in a school in Concord, across the Massachusetts state border in New Hampshire. Space travel had been her dream, and it seemed like the whole city was watching her realize it.

The launch was going to be telecast live on CNN. It was 11:38 a.m. in Concord. The teachers had put on the television in the schools. People at work had found the nearest television to watch the launch. There were roars of "Yes" when the shuttle lifted off at Kennedy Space Center. Their girl was on her way to the stars.

Then disaster struck. Only 72 seconds after takeoff, the space shuttle *Challenger* disintegrated. The entire nation, and particularly the cities of Concord and Framingham, was devastated. Teachers cried openly in front of their students, unable to control their emotions. Jennifer Peter, a reporter with the *Boston Globe*, was a high school junior in 1986. Speaking on the 25th anniversary of the *Challenger* disaster, she said, "For people who were too young to remember when JFK was shot, the explosion of the space shuttle became that moment that everyone could remember where they were when it happened." An entire nation will not be able to forget that day for the rest of their lives.

I am sure you have had similar experiences in your life where you are able to recall an incident in detail many years later. In *The Kennedy Detail*, former agent Jerry Blaine reveals information about President Kennedy's 1963 assassination. Agent Blaine was the first one to reach Kennedy's car after the shots were fired. Now in his 70s, Blaine says he still remembers the events even though they occurred 50 years ago. It is likely that someone who survived the poisonous gas leak in the Indian city of Bhopal in 1984 will remember the events of that day in graphic detail. Research studying the effects of events that produce intense emotion has shown that memories of these events, particularly national or global tragedies, are greatly enhanced. Researchers refer to the term "flashbulb memory" to explain this phenomenon. It is as if strong emotions trigger a flash of activity in the brain and every detail around us is etched in our memories for as long as the effects of the emotion last.

I like to think of it in a different way. Imagine that you are in a dark room and you cannot see anything. Now imagine that a flashbulb goes off. In the few seconds following the flash, you can see everything around you and then the darkness returns. Strong emotions have a similar effect on memory. As long as these strong emotions persist, be it seconds, minutes, or hours, every detail you observe is imprinted on your long-term memory.

Flashbulb memories are often recorded during large catastrophes or incidents of global significance. I am sure that Egyptians will remember the 2011 events in Tahrir Square in Cairo for many years to come, even if they were not actually in the square but watching the events on television or hearing about them on the radio. Flashbulb memories are also made during highly emotional events in our personal lives, like the unexpected death of a parent or child.

Both concepts, emotional memory enhancement and flashbulb memories, are fascinating for speakers because they provide a way to write and deliver memorable speeches. We will study how this can be done in Chapter 4.

Emotions Produce Actions

The power of motivation, passion, and anger to produce action has been understood and used by leaders throughout history. People at various positions have used strong emotions to align their audiences with their causes or to incite their audiences against causes. On many occasions, these strong emotions have been roused due to a well-crafted and well-delivered speech. Hollywood movies have explored the idea of an army general or king rallying his troops before battle by giving a rousing emotional speech. These themes explore the interplay between multiple strong emotions, some that are helpful and others that hurt the cause. An army of men could be roused to such an emotional state that they were willing to give up their lives for a cause greater than themselves. However, if the emotion of fear creeps into the minds of the army, it could paralyze them, leading to devastating consequences. The leader's job in this case is to understand these emotions and use his or her communication skills to arouse the right kind of emotions that would translate into effective and sometimes heroic actions.

Though strong emotion can initiate unconscious action (imagine your reflex reaction at the sound of a "hiss" behind you), our interest is in understanding the effects of emotions on conscious actions. Be it the jealous compatriot who hatches a plot to bring down his coworker or the young man in love who does unlikely things to gain the attention of a beautiful girl, people routinely do things that they otherwise would not due to strong emotions.

The second influence of emotion is in affecting our decisions. Examples of this influence is seen in television advertisements every day where the same soap could be masculine or feminine, cool or sexy, moisturizing or cleansing, and so on. Each adjective is designed to arouse certain emotions, which the advertisers hope will make us change our minds and buy their soap. Some time ago, I was asked to make a presentation at a financial conference on the subject of "Emotional Buying." The conference organizers wanted their attendees to understand how car manufacturers to jewelry sellers influence buying habits using emotional triggers. This could lead to someone buying a more expensive car to belong to a certain "elite" group even though a similar car of a different brand is available at a lower price.

In a classic example of emotional buying shown on the TV show *Nova* called "Mind Over Money," an auction was conducted for a 20 dollar bill. Interestingly, bidders became so emotionally involved with the bidding process and with each other that they were willing to pay much more than 20 dollars for the bill. You may say that this does not make any sense, but that just highlights the power of emotions.

In most cases, the effect of emotions on action and on decisions occurs at the same time. Politicians are particularly good at stoking emotions to enhance their causes. They realize that an angry or fearful electorate is likely to come out and vote. Of course, it helps if the electorate is angry with the opponent. This understanding of how emotions drive thought and action leads politicians to use divisive and sometimes inflammatory rhetoric before elections or important votes. Politicians from all parties are constantly looking for issues that can emotionally charge their base. I remember in the 2008 presidential election in the United States, there were a few conspiracy theories floating around, one of them being that then-presidential hopeful Barack Obama was not a U.S. citizen. This idea, put forward by so-called "birthers," ignited strong emotions among a small segment of the U.S. population. The opposition candidates from the Republican Party, John McCain and his running mate, Sarah Palin, further electrified their supporters by insinuating that these were valid questions and should be asked. They knew that emotionally charging the Republican base would propel them into action, resulting in more money coming into the coffers, more activists, and eventually more Republicans deciding to cast their vote.

Speakers and Emotions

How does this understanding of emotion and its influence on memory, thought, and conscious action impact speakers? Profoundly. In this era of information overload, where we are incessantly bombarded with multiple simultaneous messages, speakers are looking for ways to be remembered. The research points to working with emotions as an effective way for a speaker to be memorable.

During the Regional Ismaili Financial Conference in February 2012, there was a push to educate people on the dangers of texting while driving. The conference organizers showed a video that told the story of a young girl who had died in a car wreck that happened while she was texting as she drove. The video introduced us to her friends, the police officer who responded to the accident, and a host of other people who were affected by the tragedy. We got to know these people in the short video. We felt their loss. When the video ended with the message "Don't Text While Driving," we were all convinced.

However, there is more to this than just convincing the audience. This story itself makes the message more memorable. The video could have simply said, "Don't Text and Drive" but it took the time to connect us emotionally to the characters. The emotional connection also makes us act on the message. It is likely that many in the audience connected with the people affected by the accident and felt their loss. These audience members might decide that they "never want to feel this way" and will have a conversation with their driving-age children when they get home. The emotions aroused due to the story propel them to act.

If emotions drive us to act, then a speaker can distill the emotion that would lead to a desired action. If the speaker has identified the emotions correctly and is able to arouse them with his speech, the audience will likely perform the desired action without him even asking. The resulting action is owned by the audience, who made the decision to act without being told to do so. Such an approach is profound.

These ideas on the use of emotions in speaking are considered in the next chapter, where we discuss the emotional approach to speaking and communicating. This approach will not only provide you with a unique way of preparing a speech and making it memorable, but also, as will be shown in later chapters, develop skills in emotional intelligence, evaluation, and feedback.

Conclusions

Emotions have played an important evolutionary role for humanity. They have acted as our natural mechanism to fight danger, ensuring our reactions are quick and decisive in the face of threats. Perhaps these very reasons explain two crucial effects of strong emotions: enhanced memory and decisive action.

These two consequences of emotion are particularly relevant for speakers. Most speakers are trying to deliver memorable speeches that produce thought or action. Working with the emotions of the audience provides a unique and powerful approach to do just that. Add to this other characteristics of emotions—they are universal, are mostly independent of cultural and linguistic differences, and are experienced by the speaker and the audience—and this approach has the hallmark of being the foundation around which verbal communication should be planned and delivered.

It took me many years to understand the process of writing speeches using the emotional approach to speaking. However, looking back at those years now, I feel it was all worth it. The unquestionable power this method provides speakers is liberating as well as uplifting. And, because it works with emotions, an inherent human concept, everyone can learn to use it. Chapter 4 takes us through the process of writing and delivering speeches using emotions.

Chapter 4

The Emotional Approach to Verbal Communication

I've learned that people will forget what you said, people will forget what you did, but people will never forget how you made them feel.

—Maya Angelou

It was February of 2003. My wife and I were in San Francisco to celebrate our first wedding anniversary. Every tourist who visits San Francisco visits the waterfront attraction on the bay called Pier 39, and we were no exception. On the day we were at the pier, the weather was a balmy 70 degrees and a cool breeze was blowing from the sea. Sea lions and seals were soaking the sun all around the pier and hundreds of tourists were enjoying the beautiful day.

As my wife and I made our way toward the pier, we noticed that right at the entrance was a man sitting quietly in the corner with a leafy branch in his hand. When an unsuspecting tourist walked by, he would jump up and shout, "Boo!" You can imagine the reactions of these unsuspecting tourists. They were scared by the sudden interruption and their first reaction was to jump in fear and surprise. The popcorn in their hands would be scattered everywhere and glazed looks would cover their faces until they noticed the people around them laughing. They would catch on that this was just a practical joke. Most tourists would take it in the right spirit, considering the festive atmosphere, and just move on. Some would be irritated by the joke, or the fact that they would have to buy more popcorn, and would glare at our prankster. The joke master would apologize and smooth things out and the people would carry on enjoying the day.

In fact, it was so much fun watching unsuspecting tourists reacting to this joke that a group of 30 people or so had collected a few yards away to enjoy the reactions. Interestingly, some of the people who fell for the prankster's trick would go and join the group so that they could also get to laugh at the next victim. This went on for a while until the prankster tried his trick on a huge hulk of a man. This man was tall, strong, and at least 250 pounds, his muscles bulging everywhere. He looked like the kind of guy who could have just escaped from Alcatraz, which used to be a maximum security prison a few miles off the San Francisco shore.

The prank worked to perfection and this giant got the jolt of his life, spilled half his popcorn on the ground, and looked remarkably funny for a few seconds. Because of the size and structure of this man, the effect was a lot funnier and hence the laughs from the crowds watching were loud and exaggerated. This did not go well with the huge man who, when he realized what had happened, was not happy. The prankster meanwhile had realized how big this man was and how much trouble he was in. Seeing this hulk tower over the prankster, my wife and I were sure that the seals basking in the sun around the pier were going to get something different to eat that day. It took a lot of people and some time to calm our huge friend down, but the prankster had learned his lesson and made his way out of there.

Let's stop for a second and think about this story. Do you think the prankster could have hurt this huge man in any way? Probably not, yet the reaction of the large man was exaggerated and fearful. Do you think this big, strong man will remember this trick for a long time to come? I guarantee you that he will. For years after the incident, he probably told this story of how a crazy prankster came out from nowhere and scared him. This incident will be permanently etched into his memory.

Let's reread that last sentence: "This incident will be permanently etched into his memory." That is powerful because most speakers are trying to do just that: say something so that their messages will be etched permanently into the minds of their audiences. What can we, as speakers, learn from this incident that will help us make our speeches memorable? Once, during a workshop, I told this story and asked the above question and someone shouted, "If you want to make your speeches memorable, scare your audience to death." Although that statement is probably true, I won't recommend this approach for obvious reasons. However, the general comment has value. The reason the huge man will remember the incident for years to come is because strong emotions were generated during the incident and those emotions anchor his memories.

Most speakers dream of delivering one speech that will be remembered by their audience for years to come. The answer lies in working with the emotions of the audience. The chances are good that any speaker who leaves a strong impression on you understands the necessity of having emotions in speeches. An example of a corporate executive who understands this concept and embraces it on a daily basis is Aamir Farid. Aamir is a senior executive with Shell Oil Company, where he has to wear many hats as a communicator. Aamir wears these hats in exemplary fashion, being one of the few communicators I know who excels both in front of a large number of people and in a small, one-on-one setting.

Another extraordinary characteristic of Aamir is that his excellence in communication is very intuitive. His speeches are not deliberate or overly prepared. Aamir and I have had many discussions on what makes communication, whether it is face-to-face or a speech in front of a thousand people, memorable and effective. Through these discussions, I found an interesting similarity in our approach to communication. Even though Aamir is a natural at communication and I have had to think deeply on this topic to develop an understanding that allows me to be an effective speaker, both he and I believe that the right emotions are what make communication memorable. It is the genuine emotional connection between the speaker and the audience that makes all the difference.

Developing Speeches Around Emotions

If emotions are so effective in making communication memorable, why don't all speakers intentionally use them? In fact, most good speakers do use emotions in speeches but their approach is intuitive. Very few speakers possess the know-how to deliberately craft a speech with the emotions of the audience in mind. Realizing that emotions make a speech memorable is the easy part. Understanding where and how to use them in speeches is much more difficult. Aristotle and Churchill were considered great orators not because they used emotions in speeches but because they seemed to know when and how much emotion to use. That is what made their speeches memorable.

This understanding is not easy to develop. Earlier in my speaking forays, I did not appreciate how to write speeches with emotions in mind. In the years leading up to my 2007 World Championship win, I was working very hard to make my speeches resonate with my audience. Around 2005, I noticed a change in the feedback that I was getting from my audience. The feedback until then had been, "That was a great speech" and "You are a very good speaker." But in 2005, the feedback started to sound more and more like "You have a lot of warmth as a speaker," or "You made me feel as if I was there!"

Initially, this change in feedback was confusing. The engineer in me was used to dealing with ones and zeroes, right and wrong, good and bad. Warm did not translate very well to good and bad. Looking back, I had clearly taken a huge step forward and started connecting emotionally with my audience. It was during this time that I realized that a speech is an emotional connection with the audience and not a glib monologue using grandiose words and crisp humor that was appreciated but not remembered.

Many art forms use emotions to make their messages memorable. In the next chapter, we will discuss how some artists have used emotions to make their art memorable. It will be a revelation for you and provide you with much fodder for future speeches.

The Concept of the Final Emotion

A common source of confusion for someone beginning to prepare a new speech is "Where do I start?" The preparation of the speech begins at the end—with a clear understanding of what the final emotional state of the audience needs to be. This is the emotional state that the speaker would like the audience to be in at the end of the speech. Why is this important? In the previous chapters, we have seen that not only can emotions make messages memorable, but they also propel people to action. Because, at the end of the speech, the audience gets to reflect and resolve their emotions, their memory of the speech and their actions after it will be greatly influenced by how they feel after it's over. This makes understanding the final emotion extremely important.

Speeches, presentations, and conversations take place for a reason. In most cases, a speaker is trying to change the thoughts of an audience or make them act a certain way. Though the purpose of the speech is to influence thought and action, the speaker does not directly control the thoughts and actions of the audience. He cannot force the audience to think in a particular way or do what he wants them to do. He can only influence their thoughts or actions by making them feel a certain way so that they are likely to perform the intended action as a result of that final emotion. The concept of the final emotion provides the speaker with the closest thing to the speech objective that the speaker can directly control. It allows the speaker to work on things within his or her control and not worry about the things that he or she cannot control—the thoughts and actions of the audience.

If the speaker has correctly identified the final emotion and then delivered a speech that successfully leaves the audience with this final emotion, the audience will be influenced into thinking and acting in ways that will fulfill the objectives of the speaker.

The concept of the final emotion provides clarity for the speaker. Once the final emotion is determined, the stories, examples, and words should move the audience toward it. If this is not the case, then those stories and examples should be replaced by more relevant ones. A clear understanding of the final emotion allows a speaker to remove unnecessary components from a speech in a quick and effective manner. Frequently, the speaker will get conflicting feedback on various aspects of the speech. A clear understanding of the final emotion allows the speaker to step back and evaluate the merits of each piece of feedback.

If implementing the feedback will help in clarifying the emotional journey for the audience, helping them reach the final emotion, the feedback should be acted on. Otherwise, it is best rejected irrespective of how good it is or how much sense it makes.

The next logical question then is "How do I determine this final emotion?" The speaker should spend considerable time identifying the purpose of the speech. This requires the speaker to identify what she would like the audience to think and do after the speech is over. Remember: these are things that the speaker cannot control, but they lead to things that the speaker can control—the final emotion. Once the purpose of the speech is clear, the speaker then has to ask himself the question "How should the audience feel at the end of my speech for the purpose of the speech to be fulfilled?" The speaker is trying to identify the emotional state of the audience at the end of the speech so that the logical thought or action after the speech aligns with its purpose. This is the final emotion.

||||||||||||||||||||||||||||||||||||||||||||||||||||||||||||||||||||||||||||||||||||||||||||||||||||

The Final Emotion: World War II Memorial

Consider the example of the WWII Memorial we discussed earlier in the book. Clearly, the artist had a purpose of helping the visitors cope with their loss and helping them understand the meaning of the sacrifice made by their loved ones. The artist then determined how the audience should feel after going through the memorial. This provided him with the final emotion. This emotion is a feeling of calmness and understanding that comes from the realization that the sacrifices of the various soldiers were not wasted. The nation is a better place because of these men. It could also come from feeling proud that the sacrifices were recognized by the people of the country. These feelings form the final emotion for the artist.

||||||||||||||||||||||||||||||||||||||||||||||||||||||||||||||||||||||||||||||||||||||||||||||||||||

Going from the purpose of the speech to the final emotion is not a trivial task and may require days of introspection. The speaker has to crystallize the feelings and emotion that would lead to a certain thought and action. The understanding of the feeling should not be general but specific, allowing the speaker to feel the emotion. This clarity is necessary for the speaker to be able to transfer this emotion to the audience.

The process of identifying the final emotion and the clarity it brings to the speaking process is perhaps best shown by the experience of a young lady who attended one of my workshops. She had been recently informed that her position in her company was being eliminated. She was given a few months to find another opportunity in the company or she would have to look for employment elsewhere. The lady enjoyed working for the company and decided to explore opportunities with other divisions within it. At the time she attended the workshop, she was going around meeting managers of various divisions. The purpose of these meetings was to introduce herself and give them an idea of her skills so they could identify potential matches.

She had prepared a 10–15 minute introduction for these meetings. At the workshop, she took the opportunity to practice her introduction and seek advice on how to improve it. After she delivered her speech, it became clear that the overwhelming feeling at the end of it was that of "I have not been treated right by this company. I have worked hard and produced good results and my job is being eliminated. You should do something to correct this problem. Please try to find a place for me in your group."

This approach could have worked. She had been "unlucky" with her assignment. However, when probed further, she told us that this was not the emotion that she wanted to leave with the managers. She wanted to leave them with a more positive emotion, one that said, "I have been unlucky in the past but have managed to come out of each situation with flying colors. I am a go-getter and the kind of person that you need to have in your group."

This was a completely different emotion, probably a more powerful one. In the process of identifying the emotions that were most appropriate and aligned with her purpose (getting a job), we were able to identify the right final emotions that would make her interaction with the managers memorable and also propel them to actively search for a position for her within their group.

The second method of identifying the final emotion is by actually feeling it before you have a purpose for a speech. This requires speakers to be aware of their emotions and stopping to reflect when they feel a certain way. When a desirable emotion arises, while listening to music, watching a movie, or eating food, an emotionally aware speaker will reflect on the emotion and remember it. After the experience is over, the speaker can then choose to make his audience feel the same emotion using a speech, knowing well they will enjoy it. This determines the final emotion for his presentation or talk.

A few years ago, I experienced an emotion that I wanted to capture and share with my audience while watching a Bollywood movie called *Dil Chahata Hai* (translated as *My Heart Wants This*). The movie is about three college friends. The friends are very close but differences arise between two of them and they stop talking to each other. The differences are small and it's clear to everyone watching that it's just the characters' egos that are coming in the way. A couple of years pass and then, one day, one of the characters has a realization of how small the differences actually are. He apologizes and the three get back together.

IIIIIIIIIIIIIIIIIIIIIIIIIIIIIIIIIIIIIIIIIIIIIIIIIIIIIIIIIIIIIIIIIIIIIIIIIIIIIIIIIIIIIIIIIIIIIIIIIII

A Business Example

Consider the CEO of Company X. Company X is a large real estate firm that specializes in building affordable single-family homes. They did very well during the housing boom and almost doubled in size. The reputation was always good and they had become the builder of choice for mid-income, first-time buyers.

However, times have changed. The real estate market has collapsed and Company X, like many others in the real estate market, is having a hard time riding out the current market conditions. Company X is faring worse than some of the competition and losing market share. After a thorough review, the CEO realizes that worker productivity is low and morale of the employees is sinking. He thinks that these are the key reasons for the current problems of the company.

The CEO further analyzes the situation and finds that, though the current market conditions are to blame for some of the low worker morale, there are other reasons that are contributing to it. The CEO finds that a crucial reason for low productivity and low employee morale is that employees do not feel ownership of the organization. The CEO thinks that this may be the primary reason they may be underperforming when compared to the competition. Therefore, the CEO decides to address his speech toward developing a feeling of ownership of the company in his employees.

The CEO then thinks about the emotions that this feeling of ownership can ignite using the following basic emotions:

- Trust in the company, its management, and its values.
- Joy of being part of something that makes a difference.
- Fear of their company going under because of market competition.

How should the CEO approach his speech? How can he generate these emotions in his employees such that the torch of ownership is lit in each employee, making them improve their efficiency and hence provide the company the competitive edge it needs to survive in the current environment?

‖‖

The scene where the character realizes how small the differences are is beautifully crafted. It shows the character driving near the college campus that the three friends attended. It was here, over countless cups of tea and coffee and many interesting incidents, that their deep bond was forged. At a traffic light, his eyes wander to the campus building and he sees three students sitting at the steps of the building and laughing. He looks closely at them and sees himself and his two friends, in their younger days. At this moment, his mirror image looks up at him from the steps of the college building and just shakes his head, in regret and dismay, and then carries on with his conversation with the students sitting with him on the steps. By then, the traffic light has turned green and our character is awakened from his reverie by the horns of the cars behind him.

No words are spoken during this entire scene; however, the message is crystal clear. The image is asking the character why he let his ego destroy such a beautiful friendship. The overwhelming feeling is that the character just does not get the fact that there are few things in life as precious as good friends. To lose them over small squabbles is a mistake of monstrous proportions. Life is much more than just your ego.

The idea of the image shaking his head in dismay and looking at our protagonist is so powerful that I can never forget it. I thus used a similar idea to end one of my speeches. My speech was a personal story about how, as a teenager, I used to be embarrassed being around my grandmother. Later, I realized that I was concentrating on the wrong thing. Her love was what I should be concentrating on, not my embarrassment being around her. However, I was having a hard time ending my speech. I really liked what the director of the movie *Dil Chahata Hai* had done and wanted to leave my audience with a similar feeling. Hence, I used a similar idea to end my speech.

The Initial Emotion

If the most important step in preparing for a speech is a clear under-standing of the final emotion, another critical step is assessing the current emotional state of the audience. This assessment of the starting point of the speech is called the initial emotion. A good speaker will identify the initial emotional state of the audience and meet them at that level. This allows the speaker to form a positive emotional bond with the audience.

The initial emotional state of the audience is affected by the tempera-ment of the individual and the prevailing mood, which could be because of personal, local, or global events. The temperament of an individual is only important for a speaker in a face-to-face conversation with one or two people. If the speech is before a small or large audience, the local and global moods best describe the initial emotion of the audience. This is why good speakers do considerable research before a speech to identify events on a local scale that may determine the mood of the audience. Consider a speaker who is coming in to motivate a corporate audience. If the speaker knows that there is a restructuring effort underway at the company, which has created a climate of change and transition, he will determine that the prevailing initial emotion in the audience is that of fear and uncertainty. A good speaker will make an effort to meet the audience at that emotional level at the beginning of the speech.

In Chapter 2, we discussed the emotions that were aroused after the *Challenger* disaster. Many will also remember the speech by President Ronald Reagan that evening, delivered to console a mourning nation. It is an excellent example of a speaker who understands the initial emotions of his audience and meets them at that emotional level to start the speech. The facts associated with the *Challenger* tragedy were astounding. More than five million people had seen the *Challenger* explode on television. Some es-timates suggested that more than half of schoolchildren between nine and 13 had watched the explosion live. It was clear that this tragedy had trans-formed the mood of the entire nation from one of celebration to intense shock and loss. President Reagan knew he was addressing a devastated na-tion. This is how he began his address that evening:

> Ladies and gentlemen, I'd planned to speak to you tonight to report on the state of the Union, but the events of earlier today have led me to change those plans. Today is a day for mourning and remember-ing. Nancy and I are pained to the core by the tragedy of the shuttle

Challenger. We know we share this pain with all of the people of our country. This is truly a national loss.

Nineteen years ago, almost to the day, we lost three astronauts in a terrible accident on the ground. But we've never lost an astronaut in flight. We've never had a tragedy like this.

The first two paragraphs of President Reagan's speech tried to meet the nation at their emotional level of loss and anguish. His words, "Nancy and I are pained to the core by the tragedy of the shuttle *Challenger*. We know we share this pain with all of the people of our country. This is truly a national loss," communicated to the nation a sense of personal loss that connected him to them. It was now their loss.

President Reagan understood as a speaker that, if he wanted to take the audience to a better final emotion, he would have to understand their initial emotion, meet them at that level, form the connection, and start the healing process that would end at the final emotion.

Events in our social life, such as funerals, birthday parties, and graduation celebrations, are also examples where a speaker can make a good assessment of the initial emotion of the audience. This idea of the initial emotion is so basic that it is followed by all successful artists, be they sculptors, dancers, or speakers. Even the example we considered earlier of the WWII Memorial, allows us to estimate the initial emotion of the visitors. It is likely that visitors, particularly those who have a connection with WWII, would have an initial emotion of turmoil and loss because it is likely that most people who visit the memorial had a loved one who was lost in the war. They likely come in with some strong memories of loss and destruction, of families that were affected because of the war. The artist therefore meets the audience at that emotional state with sculptures of death and war.

In many cases, the speaker may not know enough about the audience, though every good speaker does research the audience beforehand to know the initial emotion. In such cases, the speaker can assume that the audience is emotionally neutral.

Interpreting the initial emotion in a face-to-face conversation is a little trickier. Sometimes the purpose of a predetermined meeting provides clues about the initial emotion of an individual. On other occasions, it may be necessary to spend the first few minutes assessing the initial emotion of the person. This could be achieved by interpreting nonverbal gestures, asking questions, and letting the person speak for the first few minutes to gauge the emotional state.

There are many ways a speaker can meet the audience emotionally at their level. The first, as clearly demonstrated by President Reagan in his speech to the nation on the evening of the *Challenger* disaster, is to show the audience that you are feeling the same emotions. This could happen if the speaker belongs to the same group as the audience and has been directly affected, as the audience has been, by the events around them.

In many cases, however, the speaker is an "outsider" who is not part of the audience group. The speaker here may then tap in on an emotional experience in the past to meet the audience at their emotional level. In the case of an audience whose company is going through a restructuring, the speaker could recall a time when his company went through the same and relive the emotions he felt then. A less potent version of this same technique is to recount the story of a friend or relative who went through what the audience is going through. The speaker can then form the association by recounting how he felt watching that person, his thoughts on the emotions of the person, and his acknowledgment of understanding how the audience feels now. This is not as strong an emotional connection as the speaker being able to relive the emotions of the audience, but it is better than not connecting at all.

Though it is essential for the speaker to understand the initial emotion of the audience, it is not always necessary to meet the audience at their emotional level. The speaker may choose to set the initial emotion of the audience in the first few paragraphs of her speech by starting at a different emotional state and asking her audience to join her at that state. This is particularly effective if the audience is emotionally neutral. It is common for speakers to begin their address to emotionally neutral audiences with a controversial statement, a surprising act, a humorous anecdote, or even a sentimental story. In all these cases, the speaker is setting the initial emotion for the audience.

The Emotional Journey of the Audience

Between the final emotion and the initial emotion lies the emotional journey of the audience that is the speech itself. The process of writing and delivering the speech is essentially taking the audience from the initial emotional state to the final emotional state, both of which have been determined by the speaker.

A good way to understand the emotional journey of the audience is to liken it to being led on an exciting hike by an experienced hiking instructor. Just like the instructor has a clear understanding of where the hike starts and ends, so too should a speaker know the initial and final emotion of the emotional journey that the audience is embarking upon. In the case of the hiking instructor, the student hikers meet to start the hike at a location determined by the instructor. As we have discussed, the speaker does not always have the opportunity to determine the initial emotional state of his audience but sometimes meets them at their initial state. By this time, the speaker has already determined a final emotion.

An experienced instructor will prepare and carry the necessary tools that will enable her to complete the hike. This could include ropes and other gear but also food and water. The instructor may carry flashlights and a satellite phone in case the group is lost or needs immediate help. Similarly, a speaker uses a repertoire of speaking tools to take the audience from the initial emotion to the final emotion. These tools include her speaking voice, gestures, stories, and eye contact, among others.

It will be impossible for the hiking instructor to guide the group without actually being on the hike himself. Similarly, a good speaker is only successful in taking the audience on this emotional journey by going on the journey himself. Sir Winston Churchill, considered a great orator by his peers, articulated the need for the speaker to feel the emotions that he is trying to convey to the audience. In an article called "The Scaffolding of Rhetoric," he eloquently wrote:

> Indeed the orator is the embodiment of the passions of the multitude. Before he can inspire them with any emotion he must be swayed by it himself. When he would rouse their indignation his heart is filled with anger. Before he can move their tears his own must flow. To convince them he must himself believe. His opinions may change as their impressions fade, but every orator means what he says at the moment he says it. He may be often inconsistent. He is never consciously insincere.

Sir Winston Churchill is pointing out an essential characteristic of great communicators: that unless they are also great actors, these communicators are effective because they go through the emotional journey themselves ensuring that the emotions they convey are genuine.

The hiking instructor knows and understands that hiking the sharp gradients with sudden changes in elevation are the most fun for the group. These areas offer the best views, the narrowest crossings, and the greatest rewards for the hikers. In similar fashion, good speakers understand the importance of emotional gradients in making parts of the speech memorable for the audience. These are areas that have sudden changes in emotional elevation, making it interesting for the audience. However, just like the hiking instructor understands the fun that these elevation changes bring to the hike, he also understands the need for rest after an intense part of the hike.

The ability of the group to complete the hike is reduced if adequate rest is not provided. They are also more likely to make mistakes when they are tired. Similarly, a speaker understands the need to provide "emotional rest" after an intense section of the speech. Chapter 3 discussed how strong emotions can tire an audience. A good speaker understands this and will provide rest periods for the audience, either by introducing a softer emotion like humor or by flattening the emotional gradient, to allow the audience to rest and be prepared to rejoin him for the rest of the journey.

The most confusing parts of hiking trails are when they intersect with other trails, particularly if the intersection does not have good signs indicating the right way forward. If you have ever hiked, you have probably experienced such trails. Sometimes, these intersections are so confusing that the only option is to wait for another hiker and ask for directions. An experienced hiking instructor carefully manages these intersections, ensuring that all individuals in her group choose the right way forward. She might stand at the intersection showing everyone the way forward, navigating her group through these confusing intersections. These intersections on hiking trails represent transitions in a speech. Transitions offer the audience an opportunity to take a different path and it is easy for them to get confused. Like the hiking instructor, a good speaker will manage these transitions carefully. He will ensure that the abruptness of the transition is minimized, the path forward is clearly visible, and that there is greater urgency in "sensing" the emotional engagement of the audience. If the transition is not well managed, an effective speaker will sense that he is losing the audience and will spend additional time and effort re-engaging the audience. Of course, this effort is not necessary if the transitions of a speech are well constructed.

In my workshops, I frequently tell my audience that "the best transition is no transition at all." I say this to emphasize the need to keep speeches simple. Often, speakers feel the need to use many stories and quotes from multiple sources (probably in an effort to come across as knowledgeable). These create many transitions in the speech, which, if not managed well, can lead to more problems than the solutions provided by the quotes and stories.

These concepts of reliving the emotions, emotional gradients and emotional rest, and managing emotions during transitions allow for the journey of the audience to continue without interruptions from the initial to the final emotion. This constitutes the speech experience for both audience and speaker.

||||||||||||||||||||||||||||||||||||||||||||||||||||||||||||||||||||||||||||||||||||||||||||

Learning About Transitions Through the Paintings of M.C. Escher

M.C. Escher was a Dutch artist who lived from 1898 to 1972. Escher is most remembered for painting physically impossible concepts, like water flowing uphill, without making it look unreal. The transitions in his paintings are so smooth that they do not obstruct the flow of the painting, even when it does not make sense. This allows the eye to flow from one end to the next and, soon, the viewer would be absorbing and enjoying the beauty of the painting without questioning it.

I think of Escher's uniqueness as the ability to manage transitions in paintings. In one of his famous paintings, titled *Metamorphose*, he goes from an initial pattern to various figures and shapes only to return to the same initial pattern. The transitions from one shape to the next are so smooth that the eye does not stop to question the flow. As square shape patterns turn to lizard shapes and birds turn into cities, the painting always maintains its flow. I find this remarkable painting is an excellent learning tool for speakers to understand how transitions should be constructed.

||||||||||||||||||||||||||||||||||||||||||||||||||||||||||||||||||||||||||||||||||||||||||||

The Speaking Tools

The emotional experience is delivered by the speaker using various speaking tools. Some of these tools, such as eye contact, gestures, and vocal variety, are obvious to the audience. Others, like a good introduction and a well-written biography of the speaker, are not so obvious but nevertheless help the speaker in delivering the emotional experience to the audience.

Though I dedicate an entire section of the book to tools, this is a good time to remind speakers that the speech is very different from the tools used to deliver it. As we have discussed previously, the speech is defined by the emotional experience of the speaker and his audience. Every speaker may use his or her tools differently. Some will consider vocal variety as their primary tool, whereas others use props like PowerPoint to convey most of the information. Still others will tell stories, anecdotes, and humorous jokes as tools to deliver the emotional experience.

It is important for the speaker to understand that there is no shortage of tools. If the speaker understands his emotional journey, he can use his preferred tool to take the audience on this journey. He or she does not have to be intimidated to use a specific tool just because most speakers use it. A clear understanding of the speaker tool kit and the emotional journey allows the speaker to pick up a tool that is easy to use and will get the job done.

Working With Emotions on a Macro Scale

In addition to crafting a speech that takes the audience from an initial to a final emotion, the emotional flow of the speech in a global sense can have significant repercussions to it. These macro scale emotional triggers are usually related to the construction of the speech. A speaker should frequently step back and ensure that the emotional connotations on the macro scale are aligned with the emotions that are aroused during the speech as well as with its purpose. This concept is fairly subtle and few speakers understand the influence it can have on the quality of the final emotional journey.

It is difficult to envision how a speech may arouse certain emotions just from the way it is crafted. However, it is important to align the subtle emotional messages, conveyed by the overall flow of the speech, with its purpose. If these emotions are not aligned with the goal of the speech, then the speaker confuses the audience and the speech loses its impact. This alignment could be the difference between a good speech and a great one.

As an example, consider the Bollywood movie *Rang De Basanti*. This movie follows a group of friends, all but one of whom are carefree and feel no responsibilities toward their country or community. However, one of the friends, an air force pilot, believes it is every citizen's responsibility to change their country for the better. The movie takes us through a series of incidents that lead to this group of friends caring deeply that a change is needed in their country. These friends go from feeling helpless to feeling that they can make a difference.

The viewers experience this transformation along with the characters in the film. The structure of the movie, including the cast and the state of affairs, is so different from when the movie began that it is clear that there is no going back. This emotional journey has changed the cast and the viewers. The structure of the movie aligns well with the purpose of the speech: to rise up against the state of affairs in the country. Further, the film's structure ensures that the emotional state of the audience at the end is different from when it began. This allows the director to leave the viewers emotionally energized, ready to change the pitiful conditions surrounding them. It was one of the reasons why this movie resonated with millions of people in India. There were candle light vigils held all over the country. The youth were mobilized, starting a strong campaign against corruption, which still continues to this day, albeit in a different form.

On the other hand, a motivational speaker can construct his speech to flow in the following manner: set the stage, take the audience on a journey, and then go full circle and bring the audience back to the beginning. This common approach to speech construction ties the end back to the beginning. However, consider its emotional flow. The audience at the beginning of the speech is (in most cases) neutral. They do not really know what to expect. The speaker then goes on a journey and the audience tags along for the ride. They have fun and there are parts of the speech that are captivating and motivating. The speaker ends his speech by completing the loop and bringing the audience back to where they started.

This structure throws the audience back to the emotional state at the beginning of the speech, which was neutral. Hence, the speaker has done himself a great disservice by negating the high emotions that he generated during the speech and ending it in a form that emphasizes the neutral emotional state at the beginning. This does not go well with the motivational message of the speech, which probably asks the audience to do something bigger than what they are currently doing. The motivational speaker would do well to learn from the director of *Rang De Basanti* and structure the speech such that it clearly begins and ends at different emotional states. This distinction is captured by different places, different characters (or transformed characters), different times, and so on.

This structural alignment is so rare that even some very good speeches lack it. Imagine what those speeches could have been if the emotions evoked by their structure would have been aligned with the emotions evoked by the speech itself!

Conclusions

This chapter has introduced a completely new way of writing speeches, one that emphasizes the emotions of the audience. The approach pulls together our new understanding of what constitutes a speech, which we discussed in Chapter 2, and the concepts of human emotions discussed in Chapter 3. This method is inspiring because of two reasons. First, human emotions are omnipresent. Everyone is born with them and, though some of us may be less aware of them than others, we all have the capacity to tap into them. This means we all have the inherent capacity to deliver outstanding speeches. Speakers need to work on the awareness and understanding of emotions and develop the tools that will allow them to connect and take the audience on their emotional journey. The question "Can I deliver a great speech?" is forever moot from this point forward.

The second reason for inspiration is that no one tool is a requirement to deliver a great speech. Each individual, based on personality, culture, and background, can develop a unique set of speaking tools that will enable him or her to connect with the audience and take it on this journey. This realization was very empowering, as these tools in the hands of an experienced communicator could lead to infinite possibilities.

As a further clarification of this unique method to speaking, I study various artists who have distinguished themselves in their fields. Each of these artists considers his art as an emotional experience for his audience. Each of them is communicating with us through the use of his tools. Their tools are different yet they endeavor to connect emotionally because they too believe that an emotional experience is also a memorable one. As speakers, we can learn much from studying the thoughts and methods of these artists. This is what we will do in Chapter 5.

Chapter 5

Practical Examples of the Emotional Approach to Communication

Art is about emotion; if art needs to be explained it is no longer art.
—Pierre-Auguste Renoir

The idea of working with emotions to produce a profound impact has been used in many art forms, sometimes in ways that are not obvious. Movies and music use it routinely. You may not remember the last time you were at the movies, but you may still remember the last time you got teary-eyed at the movies, even if it was many years ago. Similarly, you probably remember a well-crafted musical composition that you once heard. The music has been etched into your memory. It may be that you don't remember the exact notes and melody but you remember the way you felt at that time. You remember the emotions. Coincidently, we remember speeches in a similar way. We almost never recall the words; we only remember the emotions.

In this chapter, let's go inside the minds of other artists and find out how they go about developing a mouthwatering dish, or a phenomenal dance composition, or a breathtaking piece of music. How do they approach their art form in the emotional context? Their methods are bound to provide us with a deeper understanding of how we can write speeches for greater impact.

Renowned Chef Grant Achatz:
Using Emotions in Food

The story of celebrated Chef Grant Achatz is a revealing example of using emotions in an art form that may not seem amenable to this approach to making experiences memorable. Achatz owns an avant-garde restaurant in Chicago called Alinea. This unique restaurant serves just one menu, a 23-course meal that, on average, takes three hours to go through. In an NPR interview with Terry Gross on *Fresh Air*, Chef Achatz describes in his own words the purpose of creating such a restaurant: "So, really, what we're trying to do with that food is tell a story and craft, like an emotionally rich experience, something that makes people feel. Something that, like walking through a great modern art museum or listening to a symphony or, you know, watching a great movie or reading a great book, we're trying to do that with food."

What Achatz has been able to achieve with food is what I have tried to do with speeches. Emotions are the universal language that makes both experiences memorable. However, the tools used to achieve that emotional experience are different: I use a speech while he uses food. In the same interview with Gross, Achatz says:

> We've done food where...[it's] impaled on a burning oak leaf, oak branch, because growing up in Michigan, when I did, it was still acceptable to rake the leaves that were falling off the oak trees in your front yard out to the corner, out to the side of the road, and jump in them a couple of times. And then eventually you would light that pile on fire. And the smell of smoldering oak leaves to me is a very powerful nostalgia. It really transports me back to being eight years old and growing up in Michigan.

In many ways, Achatz's thought process is similar to what we have discussed in this book. The final emotional feeling, for example, the feeling of that happy life growing up at home in Michigan, was the starting point of a dish. Using twigs and torching the oak leaves was the process of emotionally transporting his audience back to those happy times. These tools or emotional triggers were used to achieve the final emotion.

What can we, as speakers, learn from Chef Achatz and his understanding of the power of emotions in making experiences memorable? Achatz knows that good food is a must, but what makes the food memorable are the emotions that arise when it is eaten. He is using every tool at his disposal to make that emotional experience strong, which in turn makes the food memorable. I believe this approach to cooking has many parallels with speaking.

Another takeaway for speakers, perhaps not as obvious as the first one, is the use of smell for evoking emotions. The sense of smell is the most primitive of the senses and has been shown to have a strong significance in the survival of mammals and early humanity. Thus, this sense is directly connected to the emotional center of the brain. Smells very quickly generate strong emotional responses. This scientific fact is not used often enough by speakers. When speakers use words to describe things, they describe them visually and rarely emphasize the smells and aroma associated with the visual picture. Science, and Chef Achatz's example, tells us that we should include words that emphasize smell as they can lead to a strong emotional response.

Music Maestro Ennio Morricone:
Using Emotions in Music

Ennio Morricone is one of the greatest composers to have provided music for movies. He shot to worldwide prominence for his music in Sergio Leone's spaghetti western trilogy, *The Good, the Bad and the Ugly*, *For a Few Dollars More*, and *A Fistful of Dollars*. Morricone has composed music for more than 500 movies, a staggering accomplishment. I have found his music to be emotional journeys, connecting strongly with the audience and transporting them to a very different emotional state by the end of a piece.

Morricone's work with Leone is legendary for its results. In the book *Sergio Leone: The Great Italian Dream of Legendary America*, written by Oreste De Fornari and translated by Charles Nopar, Morricone says, "Sergio generally does not even give me the script: he tells me how he feels about the characters, even the way the shots are composed. And I bring him the music." Clearly, Morricone understands that emotions create the character. His music is created to bring the feelings described by his director to life, so that the audience feels a certain way after the music is over.

In my public speaking workshops, I do an exercise to show how the power of music can change the emotions of an audience. I ask my audience to close their eyes and listen to the "The Ecstasy of Gold," a classic composition by Morricone from *The Good, the Bad and the Ugly*. The music is about three minutes and 40 seconds in duration. It starts off slowly but by the end it leaves you with a final emotion of victory and triumph. In every case, my audience is amazed at the transformation in their emotional state by the end of the music. It is remarkable how a good composer can generate such strong emotions with music.

What can we learn from the music of Morricone and other composers like him? All good pieces of music will affect the emotions of the audience. Thus, being aware of how music composers are able to transform us emotionally, speakers can observe the nuances to working with emotions. In "The Ecstasy of Gold," Morricone takes his audience up an emotional cliff in a very deliberate manner offering, on many occasions, short segments of music that seem to serve as emotional resting places. It seems that Morricone knows that the emotional transformation he is trying to achieve is too "steep." Thus, he follows bursts of emotional music by short periods of emotionally neutral music, so that the audience does not get tired. Observing a master like Morricone work with emotions is fascinating and instructional for any speaker trying to work with the emotions of an audience using a speech.

Moviemaker Satyajit Ray: Using Emotions in Movies

Satyajit Ray, a moviemaker who lived in Calcutta, India, became one of the most celebrated directors to emerge from the Indian subcontinent. Though I could have used various directors as examples in this section, Ray captures the emotions of people in a simple way, without fancy music or elaborate sets, and is able to convey them to audiences across languages, cultures, and continents. Speakers have much to learn from the genius of Satyajit Ray.

Ray's movies were known for their ability to capture realistic emotions in his characters. For the most part, he used unknown or little-known actors with minimum makeup and shot his films in natural settings. There were long stretches of pauses and his movies used very little music. This tendency toward minimal "contamination" enabled him to tell his story using the subtle emotions of his characters and their relationships with other characters. In the book *Satyajit Ray: Interviews*, he discussed his thoughts on moviemaking:

I would say that the cinema's characteristic forte is its ability to capture and communicate the intimacies of the human mind. Such intimacies can be revealed through movement, gesture, vocal inflection, a change in the lighting, or a manipulation of the surrounding environment. But there doesn't have to be literal movement at all—of the camera or the character—in a succession of shots. All the same, the character can appear to unfold and grow. To describe the most important characteristic of the film medium, I would even use the word 'growth' rather than 'movement.' The cinema is superbly equipped to trace the growth of a person or a situation. And to do that—to depict a social situation with the utmost truth and to explore human relationships to the utmost limit—one must eschew all the shortcuts that have been artificially imposed over the years by non-artistic considerations.

It was this ability to explore and capture the emotions and relationships of people that earned his movies worldwide recognition. Ray never made his movies for an international audience. His target audience was small, Bengalis living in eastern India, but his movies still found wider appeal because of his skillful use of emotion.

Ray's approach to working with emotions was authentic. His focus on taking the time to develop the emotions of his characters, their relationships with other key characters, and adding only what is required to convey those emotions should be a lesson for all speakers. Anderson Boyd, author and marketing executive, says the following on Ray's ability to work with emotions: "It is Ray's capacity to wring such intense emotion from the audience without spilling that emotion into excess—there is no catharsis here, simply the intellect coming to terms with feeling."

I strongly believe that the authenticity of the characters further accentuated the emotions and feelings of the audience, allowing them the time to enjoy and understand the emotional interplay between the characters. Clearly, Ray understood how to work with emotions in his movies.

Although Ray's approach is unique, the importance of communicating human feelings is shared by many movie directors; they are all telling their stories using emotions and relationships between the characters. There is much we can learn from Ray's methods, and those of other directors, and apply them to verbal communication. For example, there is much to be said about not overdoing things, either through words or other speaking tools.

This is often seen in the world of PowerPoint presentations where speakers have a tendency to use all the fancy tools available to them. This is a mistake and Ray shows us why. His restraint while directing and the emphasis on natural feelings, not overdone with borrowed music or hysterical acting, allows the emotions of his characters and their relationships with each other to form the core of his movies. While watching movies, I particularly look for scenes that allow emotions to develop and try to understand how the director was able to convey them.

What can speakers learn from these examples? All art forms, at their very core, work with the emotions of their audiences. Understanding how other artists work with emotions can provide great insight for speakers on how to think and plan a speech or conversation. Because emotions are universal and basic, speakers can also adapt some of the techniques used by these artists in verbal communication. The use of smell to enhance emotion by Chef Achatz, the use of emotional resting points by Morricone, and the need for authenticity by Ray are all ideas that can enhance verbal communication.

Using Emotions to Write Speeches: A Sample Speech

In a final effort to clarify this approach to communication, I will show an example that illustrates how speeches can be developed starting with the emotions that have to be conveyed. This speech, called "The Color of Love," builds on a personal experience I had when I arrived in the United States for graduate studies at Texas A&M University. I was terribly homesick for the first six months. One day in February 1996, I got up to find that it was snowing outside. Snow is rare in this part of Texas and everyone was taking advantage and playing outside. However, I found the white snow depressing and it only made me miss my family even more. My emotions were very strong that day. It seemed that, perhaps for the first time in my life, I realized the importance of my family and missed the warmth of their love. Because of the strong emotions, I remembered that day for many years and still do. When I decided to write a speech about the importance of family, I knew I had to make the audience feel the way I had felt in 1996 and take them to the same depths of anguish and longing so that they too realize the importance of family.

While working on this speech, I found it challenging to develop a good conclusion. Though I was able to capture the emotions during the speech, my ending did not capture the same depth of emotions leaving the audience feeling as if the speech could have been so much better. In short, my speech was not able to convey the final emotion effectively. I identified that the transition from the body of the speech, where I told my 1996 story, to the ending, was not allowing the emotions to flow smoothly. It was here that I borrowed an idea from the Bollywood movie called *Dil Chahata Hai* to help with the flow of emotions towards the end of the speech. (I have discussed the scene and its lesson in Chapter 4.) I think my efforts were successful because I have had attendees with tears in their eyes after listening to this speech—they often come and thank me at the end of it. This speech is a good example of how emotional awareness and learning techniques from other art forms can improve the emotional flow. You will find more examples of my speeches in the Epilogue. In each case, I explain how I approach them from an emotional view and the thoughts behind writing them. [Author's note: all ellipses in the speeches indicate a pause for the speaker.]

||||||||||||||||||||||||||||||||||||||||||||||||||||||||||||||||||||||||||||||||||||||||||||||||||||||||

The Color of Love

"Grandma, you can't do that!" I exclaimed. Grandma smiled and said, "Why, Vikas, who's going to stop me?" Well, she did have a point...nobody would dare to stop her. But I persisted: "Grandma, you can't use these combs and put them back. You have to buy them." She looked at me with those old innocent eyes and said, "Vikas, they are just lying there in a heap. I'm putting them to good use." At that point I was too embarrassed to carry on the conversation.

Ladies and gentlemen, and anyone who plans to go shopping with their grandmother, be prepared to get embarrassed because grandmothers are well beyond the age when they care about what others think of them, and when you are a teenager, that's all you care about. That summer, when I was 15, Grandma had come to visit us in Calcutta, India. On that day she had washed her hair and decided that she needed a new comb. So she came to me and said, "Vikas, let's go to the market. I don't have a comb."

Off we went to the marketplace. Marketplaces in Calcutta are something different. With the aroma of spices in the air and the clatter of rickshaws on the street, thousands of people go from vendor to vendor looking for a bargain. Here, Grandma would go to a vendor, pick up his best comb, comb her hair for a few minutes, and then calmly put the comb back and move on to the next vendor where she would repeat the process. I walked as far away from her as possible and saw the faces of the shopkeepers light up with hope as soon as my grandmother picked up the comb. Their hope would turn to excitement when they saw my grandmother comb her hair and then....she just walked away. This was just not fair.

After three hours at the marketplace, we came home...without a comb. Grandma, her hand running through her perfectly combed hair and a satisfied smile on her face, said, "Vikas, we'll go to the marketplace again on Wednesday. That's when I wash my hair again."

Grandma and I went to the marketplace many times that summer. We never bought a comb, but even as a teenager, I noticed that the marketplace was always different when I was with my grandmother. It seemed that there was more energy in the air; the people were more vibrant...as if the whole place was more colorful. This made no sense to me.

Many years later I found out that a person could indeed make a place... colorful. It was February 1996, and I had recently moved from India to Houston, Texas. It was snowing that day in Houston. Snow in Houston was so rare that the whole city was outside—playing in the snow. But I was in bed crying. I was thinking of Grandma. For the first time in my life I realized that I had always taken Grandma's love for granted. She had loved me...unconditionally...and I had not once thanked her for it. I wanted to look into her eyes and say, "I'm sorry." But she was in India...so far away.

To change my mood, I went outside. I saw the wonder on the faces of the people staring at the snow. As if the snow on the ground was nature's canvas...and they saw a beautiful picture painted on it. Why could I not see that picture? Why did the snow seem...cold...and white to me?

My thoughts drifted to Grandma and the colorful marketplace in Calcutta. I realized that I would see that picture on the snow the day Grandma would be by my side, because she would paint that picture...in the color of her love.

Too many of us live our lives in black and white. And we never get to see the most beautiful pictures in life because we fail to connect with the people around us—the very people who could paint these pictures...in the color of their love.

Now when I visit India, I try to go to the marketplace with Grandma. She still picks up those combs, combs her hair, and puts them back again. But now I walk alongside her...proudly, as if to say, "Don't mess with me...I'm with her."

And, sometimes, I just stop to observe the shops, so full of color. Once, I noticed a teenager following his grandmother and our eyes met. I felt his embarrassment. A shiver ran down my spine. What would my life be if I had never understood...the color of love?

||||||||||||||||||||||||||||||||||||||||||||||||||||||||||||||||||||||||||||||||||||||||||||||||||||||||||

Conclusions

All forms of artistic professions work with emotions. Artists may convey innovative ideas, challenge social norms, provide entertainment, or display their creations, but, ultimately, they will be remembered for the emotions they evoke in their audience. Understanding this simple idea opens the door for "cross-pollination" for a speaker. A pause in a movie can be studied for its emotional content and replicated in a speech. A few brushstrokes by a painter can be studied and ideas inferred about the visual language to use in speeches. There is an idea for the speaker in the things we do every day. The only requirements for a speaker are emotional awareness and curiosity.

Section I has provided you with an understanding of how speeches can be written starting with the emotions that need to be conveyed. Many artists, most of them unknowingly, use this approach, and excel in their chosen art form. Now we are ready to proceed to Section II, which discusses the tools that make this emotional exchange happen.

Part II

The Mechanics of Speaking

Chapter 6

Why Study the Mechanics of Speaking?

If you give people tools, and they use their natural abilities and their curiosity, they will develop things in ways that will surprise you very much beyond what you might have expected.

—Bill Gates

The excitement in the air was palpable; the audience sat quietly on neatly arranged round dinner tables awaiting the first words. The sergeant at arms had secured the door; the speakers needed no interruptions in the middle of their speeches. The rules of the contest had been read, the judges had been briefed, and the audience had been requested to turn their cell phones to vibrate. The 2006 Region VII speech contest, one of the semi-finals for the World Championship of Public Speaking, was underway. The winner of the contest would compete at the "Olympics of Oratory" later that year. The stakes could not be much higher.

The World Championship of Public Speaking, sometimes called the "Olympics of Oratory," is an annual speech contest organized by the non-profit organization Toastmasters International. At the time of writing this book, there were more than 13,000 Toastmaster clubs in 116 countries around the world. In 2006, Region VII comprised of Massachusetts, Rhode

Island, New York, New Jersey, Washington, and part of Pennsylvania. Philadelphia was hosting the regional semi-final.

Josef Martens was one of the contestants that evening, representing the Washington area. Josef was a professional speaker with an interesting background. A German immigrant, he had a PhD in physics and a knack for public speaking, two talents that rarely occur together. Professionally, he used his science background coupled with his speaking skills to help companies build a creative and innovative work culture. That evening, Josef was using a contraption as a prop in his speech, something that his innovative mind and overflowing creativity had envisioned. The audience could not have expected this to come their way.

When Josef got up to speak that evening, he had with him on stage his strange prop to help the audience understand the concept of his speech. His speech motivated his audience to keep moving in life toward achieving their goals else they stagnate and wither. But that is not why I remember the speech. To illustrate his point, Josef could have used hackneyed phrases like "a rolling stone gathers no moss." What followed, instead, was an ingenious physical demonstration of this concept using a bicycle wheel attached to a tall floor lamp stand. The lamp stand was connected to the wheel at its center in such a way that allowed the wheel to rotate without forcing it to stay upright. Josef had also built a lever that spun the wheel at considerable speed. Using this contraption, Josef showed one of the best uses of props I have ever seen in my life. He used his tool to spin the wheel, and the wheel stayed upright. Looking at the wheel spinning, erect and active, one could not have imagined that it would tilt and fall the moment it stopped. That is exactly what happened. After letting the audience marvel at the spinning wheel for a few seconds, Josef stopped the wheel and it toppled to its side, unable to maintain its balance, the upright rigidity replaced by frailty and helplessness.

I remember hearing audible gasps from the audience as they realized that physical laws, in this case the conservation of angular momentum, contained hidden lessons on life. Nature had figured out survival strategies, if only we would listen. As I sat in the audience, I was both amazed and disappointed. I was amazed because I had just seen one of the best uses of a speaking tool. But I was disappointed because I was also a contestant that day and knew that I had just heard the winning speech.

Josef had created a visual image for his audience that explained what he was saying about life. The physical principle of conservation of angular momentum is evident in many things we use, from spinning tops to gyroscopic compasses, but Josef found a way to use his understanding of this abstract law and relate it to his audience. Along the way, Josef showed me the power of the mechanics of speaking. The prop evoked strong emotions of surprise, amazement, and wonder, making his message memorable. I still remember it more than five years later!

What Are the Mechanics of Speaking?

For generations, orators have known that speaking tools in the hands of a good communicator can have devastating effects. Aristotle considered hypokrisis, or delivery, as an important tool for an orator that can be used to influence an audience. Hitler, whose ascendance to power was on the back of this speaking prowess, accompanied his speeches by "carefully rehearsed dramatic gestures" to increase the impact of the words as Dennis Glover writes in *The Art of Great Speeches: And Why We Remember Them*.

Whether it is Josef, Aristotle, or Hitler, the fundamentals of verbal communication discussed in the first section apply. The differences among the speakers arise in the techniques that they use to deliver the emotional experience to their audience. These communication tools and techniques used in verbal communication are called the mechanics of speaking. Under this umbrella fall all forms of speaking techniques and communication tools, like a person's speaking voice, vocal variety, gestures, PowerPoint presentations, stories, props, and music. Literally, everything we do that makes verbal communication possible is part of the mechanics of speaking.

This is probably the reason why there is so much confusion between the mechanics of speaking and verbal communication. The verbal communication process is an emotional experience for the audience. The mechanics enable this emotional experience by allowing the speaker to meet his audience at their initial emotion, to connect and engage them emotionally using stories and other tools, and to take the audience on the emotional journey toward the final emotion. It is a speaker's skill in the mechanics of speaking that will determine the quality of the emotional experience of the audience. In other words, the fundamentals allow a speaker to craft a speech but she needs the mechanics to deliver it.

Don't Get Stuck on the Tools

The Chinese movie *Crouching Tiger, Hidden Dragon* won many awards worldwide, including four Academy Awards in 2001, and became a box office success. Apart from fabulous martial arts and cinematic photography, this film also dealt with deep questions about life, leaving the audience with thought-provoking ideas inspired by Eastern philosophy. One such thought particularly resonated with me. In a sequence of scenes spread throughout the movie, we see the interaction between Li Mu Bai, an accomplished swordsman, and Jen, a young girl from an aristocratic family who longs for the lifestyle of a warrior. Jen steals Li's famous sword, called the Green Destiny because she believes that she can beat anyone in a sword fight if she is fighting with it.

Jen's belief is further strengthened when she is able to defeat a variety of vagabonds and warriors in sword fights, but she does not realize that she is winning these fights because of her superior skill, not her famous sword. In spite of Jen stealing his sword, Li sees her talent and wants to mentor her to hone her skill. Toward the end of the movie, Li delivers to Jen a series of lessons aimed at exposing the fallacy in Jen's approach to sword fighting. In a sword fight with Jen, Li is able to push her back despite Jen using the Green Destiny and Li using an array of makeshift swords and sticks. All along the encounter, Li explains to Jen that the foundation of sword fighting is in balance, coordination, and mental strength, not in the sword. Li suggests that a true master will be great—irrespective of the sword—because his or her foundations are strong.

Li's message should be heeded by presenters. Many novice presenters believe that the tools are the key to successful presentations, and that master presenters possess the tools that make great presentations possible. This is an error in their understanding. Great presenters are not stuck on the tools. They understand that possessing the Green Destiny does not make someone a great swordsman. Effective presenters understand the foundations of presentations and then master the necessary tools to deliver them. In the hands of a master presenter, many tools look effective because they are being used with precision to enhance communication. This sometimes generates the misleading perception that the tools are the reason for the effectiveness of the presentations.

Dana Lamon, a motivational speaker who lives in Las Vegas, is living proof that no one tool is required to deliver a great speech. Dana is blind;

he lost his eyesight when he was 4 years old. Dana cannot connect with the audience using his eyes in the traditional sense. Moreover, because he cannot see where he is on stage, Dana does not move around, preferring instead to stay at one location near something that he can touch. That is the only way he knows his bearings on stage. Yet Dana has found his way to make eye contact with the audience, using his lectern to orient himself on stage. He says:

> It has always been important to me to face the person to whom I am speaking. When I attended school and social events with other blind youngsters, I noted that some would face away from the person to whom they were speaking. I labeled that practice a "blindism" and vowed to avoid it. Consequently, I check out the speaking venue beforehand to be certain where the audience will be seated—range of seating left and right, and depth of seating. I always use a lectern, chair, or table, as a point of reference so I will always have the face-to-face orientation to the audience. Whenever I can, I have the lectern placed central to the audience to make it easier for me. I have a picture of the audience in my head. I move my body and head to the range of my audience as though I can see them.
>
> I include in my presentation material that will elicit a response from the audience. Their responses, applause, laughter, or other audible interjections, serve to re-orientate me to the range of the seating.

If Dana did not understand the fundamentals of speaking, he would be severely handicapped in delivering speeches, unable to take advantage of the two important speaking tools, namely, eye contact and stage movement. Yet Dana is able to deliver compelling speeches that keep his audience at the edge of their seats. Dana understands that speaking is much deeper than the tools. He is continuously having a dialogue with his audience, their emotional response tells him how he is doing, how connected they are, and if they are coming along the emotional journey with him. Dana says: "The responses, applause, laughter, and other audible interjections mentioned above for orientation, also let me know if my audience is with me, if they are following me, and how they are connecting emotionally with me."

Dana's approach is remarkable because he is unconsciously doing what *Emote* is recommending. He understands that many tools can be used to deliver similar emotional experiences to the audience. A skilled speaker like Dana understands how a particular tool enables a deeper emotional experience for his audience and, if that tool is not available, figures out a "fix" or another tool that works well for his situation. The important thing is always enabling a deeper conversation with the audience, not the tool.

The fundamental understanding that no one tool is essential to be an effective communicator will fill you with confidence. It will provide hope to the hesitant immigrant who has a slightly squeaky voice, and believes that a loud, booming monotone is essential to deliver memorable messages. The shy introvert will gleam with delight when she realizes that irrespective of what she has been told, using large gestures and movements on the stage are not the only ways to impact an audience. It will spur them both to identify their preferred tools and develop a toolkit that will enable them to communicate effectively.

Different Strokes for Different Formats

Mechanics are also the reason why few communicators are good at different communication formats. I remember meeting a leader in my organization who was mesmerizing in a one-on-one conversation. He used a soft yet determined voice to connect, and interesting tidbits and vignettes to keep attention, and provided life lessons in an unassuming manner to motivate. The dialogue was fascinating, leaving me scratching my head as to why this leader was not higher up on the corporate ladder, given his strong technical reputation and many years of experience.

Sometime later, however, I had an opportunity to see this leader deliver a talk in front of a group of people. On this occasion, his soft voice accompanied by the small gestures did not engage the audience. Many in the back row were straining their ears to understand what this leader was saying. The "no drama" manner in which the vignettes were delivered, including no vocal variety or movement, did not provide the excitement to engage a large audience. At the end of the presentation, I was disappointed by the lack of energy and motivation. I understood why the leader had not progressed further in the organization, since the ability to engage large audiences becomes increasingly important with increased corporate responsibility.

Most people have a default speaking style. This is the style that comes naturally, allowing them to engage their audience emotionally and to be an effective communicator by influencing thoughts and delivering memorable messages. The single biggest reason why many communicators who are effective in their default settings fail in a different communication setting is that they use the same tools to convey emotion. Typically, these speakers do not understand the fundamentals of verbal communication. They naturally convey emotions in their default communication style but appear lost when the communication settings change. In most cases, they are not aware that a different toolkit may be required for different verbal communication formats. As a consequence of this lack of awareness, they have never taken the time to develop a robust toolkit, with tools suited for different communication formats. Such speakers are ill-prepared to take their audience on an emotional journey when the communication format changes.

A great communicator knows his default communication format. Certain tools, which are suited to his default style, come naturally and effortlessly to him. However, he understands the need to develop tools better suited for other verbal communication formats. He knows that the tools used to convey emotions in various communication settings may be different. Because he understands the foundations of verbal communication, he picks and chooses different tools, based on his communication style, personality, and environment, when the communication format changes. Though an effective speaker should have a variety of tools in his toolkit, he or she does not have to learn and master all the tricks, as preached by some communication coaches.

Let's look at some specific examples where tools that are effective in one format of verbal communication create problems when used in another verbal communication format.

- The use of vocal variety: Vocal variety is used extensively by public speakers to express emotion to their audiences. A loud, deep voice can express anger. A soft, deep voice can express fear, and a high tempo, fast-paced approach can convey excitement. However, too much vocal variety in a small setting is usually not effective. In small settings, the variations in vocal variety need to be small. Due to the intimate nature of the setting, these small changes are enough to convey emotions. In fact, a large range of vocal variety in a small setting will be a distraction rather than an asset.

- Using gestures: In a conversation with a small group of people, such as a roundtable conversation, using small gestures at appropriate times can add emphasis and strength to your points. Shaking of the head to indicate agreement or disagreement during a conversation is also a common method in small settings. However, small gestures are not effective in large settings. Here, large hand movements to indicate preference and exaggerated facial movements to indicate agreement will work better.

Conclusions

Most authors who write about verbal communication end up writing about the use of tools. This has resulted in a plethora of books that discuss the mechanics of speaking, providing ample knowledge and examples on the use and nuances of many speaking tools. Knowing this, I have stayed away from discussing each of the tools in excessive detail. Consider this to be an awareness section, where I discuss the use of a tool in enabling the emotional experience, then distill the knowledge from the most popular books on each skill, and present it to you. On this background, I overlay my experience and knowledge from years of speaking to provide practical examples and interesting facts. Finally, I include a detailed list of references in the Bibliography that allow an interested reader to research each tool and, coupled with practice, develop a mastery of that communication tool. The results are concise sections on each speaking tool, providing an understanding of when and why to use one.

Chapter 7

The Words

*If you would be pungent, be brief, for it is with words as with sunbeams—
the more they are condensed, the deeper they burn.*
—Robert Southey

It is difficult to imagine President John F. Kennedy's inauguration address having the same impact on the entire population of the United States without the words, "Ask not what your country can do for you; ask what you can do for your country." These words became the symbol of what JFK stood for and galvanized an entire nation. They became the rallying cry for a young president and represented the "sacrifice for your country" attitude that he was putting forth.

President Kennedy's speech, as well as many other famous speeches, indicates that words can have a huge impact on people. Periodically, a phrase here or there catches the imagination of people, spreads like wildfire, and seems to be on the minds and lips of everyone around us. More often, however, a poor choice of words is flashed repeatedly in the media. It is common to see speakers on television explaining or apologizing over using the wrong word or using them poorly. All this leads us to believe that it is paramount that the perfect words are used in a speech. In fact, it is commonly believed that a great speech consists of great words spoken at the perfect time.

This is one of the greatest myths in public speaking. For many years I, like many others, believed that the right choice of words could make all the difference in my speeches. My belief was that if I could say the right words at exactly the right time, I could make a profound impact on people. This thought process made me focus exclusively on the words, continuously looking for ones that were "perfect" for the moment. The problem, as you can imagine, was that it is extremely difficult to determine when the right moment is for a particular word. The search for the right word made me focus on myself and my thoughts, taking me away from the real soul of a speech, the connection a speaker has with his or her audience. The fallacy of focusing on the words is pointed out by Dale Carnegie, a public speaking pioneer, who writes in his book *The Quick and Easy Way to Effective Speaking*: "The man who writes out and memorizes his talks is wasting time and energy, and courting disaster. All our lives we have been speaking spontaneously. We haven't been thinking of words. We have been thinking of ideas. If our ideas are clear, the words come as naturally and unconsciously as the air we breathe."

I now realize that words are not the most important part of the speech. In fact, words are only a tool used by the speaker to deliver an emotional experience to her audience. I now believe that the audience members will only recall a few words the speaker says, but they will remember how the speaker made them feel.

This concept, that perfect words are not required in a speech, is empowering. It means that the speaker need not be worried about the exact words in his speech, but only about the emotions he is conveying. This concept confronts the fear of public speaking at its very root. Speakers, who have dreaded speaking because of a fear of forgetting the words of their speech, suddenly realize that they have been worrying about the wrong thing. The exact words will have minimal impact. They just need to convey their feelings and emotions.

I do not want to disregard completely the importance of words in a speech. Some words allow for a better flow of emotions than other synonymous words. In this context, the choice of words in a speech can make a difference. Poor choice of words can disrupt, or hinder, the flow of emotion from the speaker to the audience. For example, words or phrases that do not make sense will inevitably cause the audience to ponder what is being said, causing them to disengage from the emotional connection with the speaker. As long as the flow of emotion is uninterrupted, the exact words are not important. The words used in a speech are a tool to transfer these emotions and, once they are transferred, the words become irrelevant. With practice, speakers can develop a strong awareness of how their speech is flowing and identify words that are disrupting that flow. These words can then be replaced with others that do allow the speech to flow better.

If you have ever cried while watching a movie in a language you do not understand, you know exactly what was said in the previous paragraph. Movies, like a speech, are an emotional experience. As long as the viewer understands the feelings and emotions of the actor, the movie has been a success. This is also why eloquence in speaking does not automatically translate to maximum impact on the audience or vice-versa.

I recently heard a speech by a colleague who delivered an emotional appreciation for his parents and their sacrifice to help him succeed. He spoke about their journeys as they entered the United States illegally from Mexico, looking for a better future. He talked about their struggles as they lived without their children in a foreign land, only to ensure that their children had more opportunities than they did. His speech was powerful, emotional, and impactful. My colleague's speech had many long pauses while he searched for words: his choice of words could have been better, and his grammar was awkward on occasions. But his emotions came through loud and clear. My colleague showed that sometimes speakers who have a tough time putting proper sentences together are still able to deliver powerful, life-changing speeches because they provide emotional experiences for their audiences. As long as speakers are able to connect with their audiences and convey their feelings and emotions, they can deliver great speeches.

How then can we make sense of the multitude of politicians and celebrities routinely appearing on television to explain what they meant when they used a certain word? This seems contradictory to what I have discussed earlier. However, consider the following question: what if I did not hear a speech in person but heard a taped version of it? I was not there to "feel" the emotions of the speaker, the context, and the ambiance that existed when the speaker was on stage delivering her speech. In such a situation, I would have to infer the context and emotion of the speaker from the words of the speech. I will play or read the words again and again, and try to determine what the speaker was thinking, what she was feeling, and analyze why certain words were spoken. In this situation, and others like it, words are important.

When speakers are in front of the media or are making presentations that are being recorded and analyzed by individuals who did not hear the original speeches, words do carry greater significance. Because the people listening to recorded versions of the speeches did not feel the speakers' emotions, they tend to give greater emphasis to the exact words used by them in an effort to understand the emotions and thoughts being conveyed. This is a difficult task and likely to lead to inaccurate conclusions regarding the spirit of the speakers' comments.

This struggle is clearly visible when politicians make speeches. Invariably, every word in their speeches is dissected and discussed by people who were not present to listen to them in person. Sometimes these analysts do not take the time to listen to the full speeches, instead drawing conclusions only from snippets and clips. Though the comment "my speech was taken out of context" has become a hackneyed phrase used by politicians to change their stated position when it goes against popular beliefs, in many cases the spirit of their speech was indeed not accurately captured by analysts who are focusing too narrowly on the words. This has led to the culture of public figures reading scripted speeches using teleprompters. Unfortunately, the ability of such scripted speeches to make a deep emotional impact is minimal.

Word Constructs Help the Flow of Emotions

Speakers can use certain techniques to convey emotions more effectively using words. Some of these techniques follow.

Using Visual Words

Research has shown that data presented as visual images is remembered better than the same data presented in numerical or auditory form. In some interesting research on a concept called "Picture Superiority Effect" cited in the book *Universal Principles of Design*, people recalled advertisements better when they had text and pictures rather than pictures alone. The speaker can use this understanding to her advantage by using words that paint visual images in the minds of her audience.

I have routinely used words to bring my characters to life. Consider the following paragraph from my award-winning speech, "The Swami's Question." Here, I introduce the Swami to the audience.

One afternoon, Mom and I traveled to the old part of the city of Calcutta, India. Here, the houses were so close that sunlight was a myth. The aroma of spices drifted in the hot, humid air and in a small hut sat the holy man everyone called the Swami. His saffron robe drenched in sweat, he tried to solve the problems people put before him.

Notice how I use words to bring in the senses of smell, color, and touch to paint a graphic image of the Swami and his adobe. This allows the audience to build a visual image of the Swami in their minds. They imagine his face, his clothes, his small hut, and the environment around him. This image may not be exactly the same as the image the person next to them has created, but that is not important. The fact that they now have a visual image of the Swami has made the character more memorable.

Use of Poetry and Rhyme

Using sentences that rhyme, or the use of poetry in a speech, can be an effective tool for a speaker. The audience will not remember the exact words that were used in the poem or rhyme, but poems have a way of helping the flow of emotions. William Wordsworth, a famous British poet, called poetry "the spontaneous overflow of powerful feelings" in his essay "Preface to Lyrical Ballads." If a speaker can share this "package" of emotions with the audience by using a poem in an appropriate context, it will make for an effective mechanism to transfer emotions.

On a similar note, it is also common for speakers with a good singing voice to sing a few lines of a song as part of the speech. The reasons songs are effective in a speech are similar to the reasons why a poem is effective in one. Songs are a very efficient way to transfer emotions. A good singer can move an audience by singing just a few lines of an appropriate song. I remember witnessing the 2008 World Championship of Public Speaking in Calgary, Canada. The winner that day was the late LaShunda Rundles, an African-American woman from Dallas, Texas. LaShunda was also a wonderful singer, with a voice that carried a lot of emotion. She used her singing voice to great effect in her winning speech, using it to form a strong emotional connection with the audience. It was an excellent example of how singing can be incorporated in a speech to enhance its impact.

Conclusions

Words are an important tool used by speakers to convey information and emotion. Though it is common for people to dwell on famous words spoken by leaders and communicators, the real test for whether the right words were used is if they conveyed the information and emotions of the speaker. If the right emotions and information were conveyed, then the order of the words is not important. It can be argued that many different arrangements of words could convey the same emotions and information. All these word arrangements are valid.

The sequence of words can impact the effectiveness of a speech. Certain constructs of words, like poetry or alliteration, allow for emotions to flow better in a speech. Such constructs should be used by speakers when appropriate to enhance the impact of their speeches.

Related to the words used by the speaker, a speaker's voice is also a medium used to convey emotion. Chapter 8 discusses this speaking tool in more detail.

Chapter 8

Using Your Voice

O, how wonderful is the human voice! It is indeed the organ of the soul!
The intellect of man sits enthroned visibly upon his forehead and
in his eye; and the heart of man is written upon his countenance.
But the soul reveals itself in the voice only.
—Henry Wadsworth Longfellow

A speaker's principal tool to communicate emotion is his or her voice. The voice is a particularly effective tool in communicating emotion because of the variety that can be achieved by varying pitch and volume. Have you noticed that we tend to associate emotion with a particular type of voice? For example, a shrill loud voice, a shriek, is associated with extreme fear or anguish.

A speaker's voice is the equivalent of a guitar for a musician or paint for an artist. However, effective use of the voice to communicate emotion requires skill, practice, and, above all, an understanding of how emotions are communicated using the voice.

As with a musician playing his instrument, a speaker has the opportunity to use his voice to engage an audience with humor, to capture the excitement of seeing a cheetah in full flight, or to communicate the wonder of an awe-struck child. Yet most speakers rarely use the range, variation, depth, and distinction of their voices to communicate these emotions.

As part of my workshops, I often play a few pieces of music for my students. While the music is playing, they are instructed to close their eyes. When the music stops, I ask them to keep their eyes closed and I'm aware of the emotions that they are feeling. Afterward, we have a discussion where they share their emotions and the visual images that they imagined while the music was playing. The results are almost always astounding, with images described in graphic detail and strong emotions being felt at the end. It is amazing what a good piece of music can do.

All of us have been through similar situations in our lives. When we are angry, we raise our voices. When we get excited, we cannot say things fast enough. Sad emotions usually result in measured words in a soft voice. Yet we fail to understand that our tempo and volume convey emotion in our speeches. Few speakers consciously synchronize their voice and their emotions.

This is primarily because speakers are not feeling the emotions of their speeches. If the speaker does not feel the passion he is trying to convey, his speech will not adequately convey these emotions. However, if the speaker feels the passion in her words, her tempo and voice will automatically move toward the region where they convey these emotions. If the speaker feels the anger in his speech, he will raise his voice without thought or effort. It will be a natural reaction.

Here, however, is a word of caution. I mentioned earlier that the vocal tone and tempo will automatically move toward the sweet spot that will convey the intended emotions effectively. This does not mean that they will hit the sweet spot. The speaker then has to introspect, through feedback and awareness, as to what changes need to be made to convey the emotions effectively. A speaker, for instance, may need to slow down an angry outburst or lower his voice for a small-sized room. The speaker has to be aware of his default tempo and tone that is associated with anger, which he projects to the audience in his speech. It need not be the most effective pace and tempo to convey emotion. In my experience, starting from the default tempo and pace that one associates with the emotions, is a good place to begin. A good speaker, working with a mentor and using feedback, can then develop the correct tempo and volume that work for that speech. A speech, ultimately, is for the audience and not for the speaker.

Your Resonant Voice: The Key to Voice Projection

In physics, resonance is an inherent property of a system where, when certain conditions are met, it is able to capture energy from the environment. This energy is then manifested in large motion or loud sound.

The human voice is also a system with a resonance property. Most speakers, however, never fulfill the conditions that will allow for the sound to be resonant. The advantage of a resonant voice is that it projects very well. The speaker doesn't have to shout to be heard in a large room; his voice travels clearly and crisply to all locations.

In my presentations, I often get asked about voice projection. There are two main reasons why a speaker has trouble projecting his voice. First, he is nervous. Our vocal cords have been generated for our special voice and work best when they are relaxed. In this situation, our voice has a distinct edge; it is resonant and carries far without effort. However, when we are nervous our muscles are tense and the voice we generate is not our resonant voice. In such situations, we have to make a considerable effort to be heard. Further, the voice seems forced and gives a disingenuous feel.

Second, the speaker has not experimented with the resonant voice. Once she understands her voice a little better, she can then develop it to be resonant, and it will project much better. Most speakers are so tense before their presentations that their muscles do not relax and they do not speak in their natural voice. It takes them a considerable amount of effort to speak up and be heard.

The best way to discover your resonant voice is by doing vocal exercises specifically designed to improve your resonant voice. I often sit down in a quiet room and chant "ohm," an ancient Sanskrit sound. The sound "ohm" is usually associated with meditation. The chant initially originates at the naval and, as the chant progresses, the original point of the sound propagates upward. The final part of the chant comes from the head. This chant has worked well for me and helps me develop my resonant voice.

The Pitch, Tone, and Volume of Speaking

The pitch of a voice is a quantitative measure of frequency of the sound generated. Pitch does influence emotion. When the body is stressed, as with the emotions of fear, anger, and excitement, the pharynx is smaller and the vocal cords produce higher-pitched sounds. Similarly, when the body is relaxed, as with love and joy, the voice muscles are relaxed, producing lower-pitched sounds.

Volume also has an effect on emotion. Higher volume is associated with higher energy and is important to convey the emotions of excitement. Low volume conveys calmness.

Finally, the tone of the voice is an important indication of emotion. Two people can have the same pitch and volume but a different tone and, so, convey different emotions.

Use of the Pause

The pause can be a very effective tool for a speaker, yet it is difficult and often awkward to use. Still, its power has been felt by all of us, even if unintended. I was fortunate to see the immense power of the pause recently. I was invited to be a judge in a speech contest at a local school. The kids were aged 8 to 16, and enormously talented. However, the incident that stands out in my mind from that day is when one of the younger kids got up to deliver his prepared speech. He had obviously memorized his speech and showed all the signs of nervousness that we often see in speakers. About a minute into his three-minute speech, he forgot the words. For the next 30 seconds, he looked at the floor, too scared to make eye contact, trying to remember what he was to say next. What I saw in those 30 seconds boggled my mind. Unlike all the others in the audience, I had taken the liberty to look at the audience and not the speaker, trying to gauge their reactions. I saw that people watched in rapt silence, their complete focus on this child. If they had been thinking about other things before, those thoughts were gone. I saw the kind of attention given to this young boy that is reserved for the very best speakers. I heard the kind of silence in the room that any speaker in the world would drool over. I heard the power of a pause.

Sure, you might say that the audience was sorry for this kid, and that partly explains the silence. I agree. My point, though, is that sometimes a pause can grab and keep an audience more powerfully than any words you can say. Speakers need to understand and appreciate the sound of silence.

I have found immense clarity with when and how to use the pause by using the premise that the speech is not a monologue but a dialogue. For instance, should a pause be required after a speaker asks the audience a question? Clearly, in a dialogue, a question will be followed by the answer from the person(s) to whom the question was addressed. It would be considered rude to interrupt that answer, and the questioner should stay silent until the question is answered. In a speech scenario, this is still true. An audience normally responds to the question put forth by the speaker not verbally but in their mind. The speaker would do well to give them a few seconds of silence while they answer his or her question. I would ask you to consider the premise that a speech is a dialogue, whenever you are in doubt of the duration and location of a pause in your speech. It will provide you with immense clarity.

The movie *The Great Debaters* offers an exquisite example of how a pause can generate strong emotions in a speech. The movie follows a debating team in a small, black college as they, under the leadership of their charismatic coach, have an undefeated season. In the final act, they get an opportunity to debate the mighty Harvard University debating team. It is during this debate that this scene occurs. The Turner College debaters have put forth their points; Harvard has delivered its reply. Now it is the turn of Turner College. Their debater gets up and walks to the podium. He is obviously nervous. This is a big moment. For what seems like the next minute, he does not speak. The silence is deafening. His family is listening to the debate on the radio in Texas and his little sister, after what seems an eternity of silence, jumps up and shouts: "Why does he not say something?"

When the debater starts speaking, he talks about how he and his teammates saw a man being lynched, their feelings, and their fear. He makes the point that no man should be treated this way and it is their duty to resist such oppression. He ends by saying, "It is my duty to resist by violent means or non-cooperation. You should pray I choose the latter," to great applause.

What this debater was able to do was understand the emotional content of his speech and then use the pause to accentuate that emotion. The contents of his talk would make anyone uncomfortable. Talking about lynching in the northeast in a room filled with Caucasian Americans was going to be difficult. He therefore used silence to set the stage. His silence was so long that it made people uncomfortable, preparing them for the uncomfortable words that followed. It is a beautiful example of the power of the pause and exemplifies the use of speaking tools to affect the emotions of the audience.

Using Your Accent

I have an accent. It is a little less pronounced than it was when I came to the United States in 1995, but I still have one. There are millions of people, particularly immigrants, who speak with an accent. There is no reason to worry. Consider walking into a store and seeing something unique that is not commonly found in your area. It would catch your eye and you would spend a little time looking at the object and thinking about it. An accent works the same way. For a speaker, an accent can be her biggest asset, if she knows how to use it. An accent sets a speaker apart immediately. It builds interest from the first word, and the audience is eager to find out a little more about the speaker and listen to her perspective.

However, one does need to be careful if you are not a native speaker of the language. First, it probably is not prudent for you to speak at the same pace as a native speaker because, though your audience is enjoying your accent, it is also taking a little more time to comprehend what you are saying. This is usually because you pronounce words differently, but also because you may use different ones than those commonly used by native speakers. Second, some languages do not have all the letters of the English language. Sometimes, they have more. In either case, what comes out of your mouth when you pronounce words with these characters will be difficult to understand for a native speaker. It is useful to be aware of specific words that you pronounce very differently from native speakers, and either slow down when you say them or use different ones instead.

I would like to emphasize that I consider my accent to be an asset. I never try to "put on" an accent to mingle with the crowd or be perceived as a native. I would rather be very comfortable when I am communicating than be stressed while trying to say things in a way that is not normal for me. That being said, I have understood that my accent makes it difficult for me to do certain things, such as speak quickly. I therefore work within this framework, always keenly aware of the expressions of my audience so to make sure that they understand what I am saying. If I do this, I usually enjoy the benefits of having an accent—immediate interest in what I am saying.

Conclusions

A speaker's voice is an excellent tool to convey emotion. The pitch, volume, and pace of the speaker's voice convey emotions. It is important for a speaker to make sure that these emotions are congruent with those conveyed by the words being used. The pause is an effective, but often underused, part of vocal variety that should be explored in greater detail by speakers.

The voice of a speaker can also convey information about the background of the speaker. This could be in the form of an accent or the pronunciation of the words. Although an accent can create a lot of interest, it can also disrupt the emotional journey of an audience if the words spoken by a speaker are not understood by the audience. It is best for a speaker with a heavy accent to slow down to provide time for the audience to understand his or her words.

Apart from words and voice, a speaker has many nonverbal tools to convey emotion. These include gestures, props, and stage use, among others. A skilled speaker will understand the use of these nonverbal tools and use them to enhance the emotional experience of the audience. We will further study these nonverbal tools in Chapter 9.

Chapter 9

Nonverbal Communication: Gestures, Props, and Stage Use

What you do speaks so loud that I cannot hear what you say.
—Ralph Waldo Emerson

Most speakers do not realize the power that their gestures have in diluting, confusing, or negating their messages. On the other hand, speakers who use gestures effectively enhance their core messages by opening up another channel of communication with their audiences. They use gestures to fortify and bolster their verbal massages.

I once saw Craig Valentine, the 1999 World Champion of Public Speaking, do a fun exercise that illustrated the importance of gestures. I liked it so much that I have used (with his permission) a similar exercise in my workshops. I ask my audience to stand up but make sure that they can see me. I then ask them to do exactly as I say. What follows are a series of commands like "Put you left hand on your right hand," and "Put your right hand on your left elbow."

I demonstrate each command with action, where I perform the gesture that I am asking my audience to perform. The last of the series of commands usually ends by saying, "And then put your right hand on your right cheek" but I intentionally put my hand on my chin. It is amazing to see how the audience responds. I find more than 50 percent of the audience with their hands on their chin even though I had asked them specifically to do as I say. That is the power of gestures!

This exercise embodies an important aspect of how messages are absorbed by our brain. Research has shown that visual images stimulate the brain at a greater extent than auditory messages. In the previous exercise, the audience received contrary information from visual and auditory communication channels and, because the visual channel is stronger, they assumed that I had erred in saying what I intended them to do. Their immediate reaction was to believe my actions. The challenge for any speaker is to ensure that actions, gestures, props, and stage use are aligned with his words. Any discrepancy would cause confusion in the audience.

‖‖‖

Nonverbal Cues Make a Difference

During the 1960 U.S. presidential election, the first debate between Richard Nixon and John F. Kennedy offered a stark reminder of the importance of nonverbal communication. On the day of the debate, Nixon was ill. He used no makeup for a televised debate and wore a pale suit that further accentuated his pale skin color. He looked tired and sapped of energy. On the other hand, Kennedy wore a dark suit, which contrasted well with his fair skin. He used makeup and had spent several hours before the debate practicing his delivery and gestures. Most people who heard the debate on the radio thought Nixon had won but an overwhelming majority of the people who watched it on television said that Kennedy was the winner. Nonverbal messages, in this case, helped Kennedy with the presidential debate.

‖‖‖

This chapter covers the three main ways in which a speaker communicates nonverbally: gestures, props, and stage use. Each of these is related, but different enough that they can be treated separately.

Gestures

Gestures are movements of any part of the body that are used as an expression of a thought. These typically involve the movement of the arms or the use of the hands to express or emphasize an idea or thought. Most of us use gestures on a daily basis without giving it much thought. However, improper gestures during speeches can have negative consequences. In my workshops, a common question I get asked is, "What do I do with my hands when I am speaking?"

Speakers worry they may be doing something inappropriate, like moving their hands too much while they are speaking, which may be distracting for their audience. They are correct in trying to identify and remove gestures that are distracting but do not realize the underlying problem. If a speaker feels that her hand gestures are inappropriate, the thought makes her uncomfortable. Unfortunately, even if the audience is not distracted by the speaker's gestures, they feel the speaker's discomfort and become uncomfortable also. Thus, in most occasions, the speaker being uncomfortable causes more problems than the gesture itself.

IIIIIIIIIIIIIIIIIIIIIIIIIIIIIIIIIIIIIIIIIIIIIIIIIIIIIIIIIIIIIIIIIIIIIIIIIIIIIIIIIIIIIIIIIIIIIIIIIIIIIIIII

Confusing Visual Cues

Conflicting messages conveyed by signs and visual cues are common in society. Consider a door with "PUSH" written on it, but also with a door handle that allows it to be pulled. The "PUSH" sign indicates that the door will open when pushed but the presence of a door handle is a strong visual message that we need to "PULL" this door to open it. In many instances, a person will believe the visual cue as accurate and assume that the text on the door is an error. Consider what this means when your gestures contradict your words.

IIIIIIIIIIIIIIIIIIIIIIIIIIIIIIIIIIIIIIIIIIIIIIIIIIIIIIIIIIIIIIIIIIIIIIIIIIIIIIIIIIIIIIIIIIIIIIIIIIIIIIIII

Many gestures, though they do not add to the speech, also do not distract from it. One way to identify distracting gestures is feedback from the audience on which gestures they remember. An approach to using gestures is that they are tools that help the audience in their emotional journey, which is the speech itself. If a particular gesture or prop stands out, then the audience members stop to think about it. They ask themselves, "Why is he doing that?" or "What does that prop mean?" The questions that they have in their minds are not important. What is important is that for a few seconds the speaker has lost his audience and they are no longer on the emotional journey.

Another way to identify inappropriate gestures is to videotape your speech. Distracting gestures are easy to identify while watching a video. However, I do have a word of caution when using video to improve speeches. It is easy to be too critical of yourself while watching a videotaped speech. If you identify certain gestures that are distracting, they should also be reflected in feedback from the audience. In many cases, the problem is perceived but not real.

Videotaping a speech can provide opportunity for speech enhancement by aligning the gestures with its message. One idea is to watch the speech on mute. Can you identify the story just by looking at the gestures, facial expressions, and movement? Is the nonverbal message different from the verbal message? If so, you will know which gestures are inappropriate and how to align them with the verbal message.

An advanced speaker will take this a step further. She will identify areas in the speech that are confusing or need clarification. She will then try to identify gestures that will provide nonverbal clarity to the words and plan to use these gestures at appropriate points in the speech. Many advanced speakers write their speeches with two columns (see the following figure), the first with the words that make up the speech itself and the other with the gestures that go with those words.

Speech	Gestures
Speech	Associated gestures

Props

Props are similar to gestures except the speaker does not use a part of his body but an external object to visually communicate with the audience. A prop could be anything: a piece of clothing, a picture, or even an envelope, which is what I used in my World Championship speech.

Props, like gestures, are primarily used to bolster the verbal message. A good prop can communicate in ways that are difficult for words to describe. During a speech, a speaker used a black cloak to indicate adversity. He had struggled with a speech impediment for many years and was able to overcome it. He used the black cloak to cover himself on stage, an indication of the dark days he had gone through and then threw off the cloak and appeared with his chest out. The symbolism of him breaking free and seeing the light was powerful, emphasizing his victory over his disability in a way that would have been difficult to say using words.

The use of props does need careful planning. A prop is an external object that is brought into the speech to serve a specific purpose. After the purpose has been served, it needs to be removed so that the audience can move on with the emotional journey. Consider a speech by an astronaut where she uses a piece of the moon that she brought back from her moonwalk. Though this prop serves a very important purpose—it indicates that "I was there," and the emotional impact is tremendous—the audience is lost during the time the prop is in front of them. They are busy analyzing the prop or figuring out some other detail about it. The speaker needs to give them time for the emotions to sink in, ask and answer questions they have, satisfy their curiosity, and then remove the prop from their sight so they can get back on the emotional journey.

This action of removing the prop after its purpose has been served could be the determining factor, in some cases, of the appropriateness of a prop for a speech. In my championship speech, I used an envelope as a prop. Initially, I had thought about opening the envelope, removing the letter inside, tearing it up, and throwing the pieces in the air. The small pieces falling all over me would make a powerful impact, aligned with what I was saying, on the audience. However, I was then left with a difficult task of removing the small pieces so that I could move on, or leave the pieces on the floor, which would have distracted the audience. In the end, I decided to just show the closed envelope and let the audience imagine the letter inside. My prop was a little less powerful but was more effective as a "tool" for the speech.

Even after this decision, the process had to be further streamlined before it could be used. The envelope remained inside the pocket of my suit jacket until I needed it. In my practice sessions, I was not having any problems taking out the envelope, but putting it back into my suit pocket was difficult without stopping and concentrating on the act. This took away from the emotional experience of the audience as they stopped to watch me struggling to put the envelope back into my pocket. I was able to sew a large pocket on the inside of my suit so that I could put the envelope back with ease.

A good prop can have a strong visual impact on the audience and bolster the message of the speaker. It is a tool that all speakers should utilize when appropriate.

The Use of the Stage

"I could see the Swami on the stage," said someone who had come to congratulate me after my win. In my speech, I had created a "space" for the Swami, a character in my speech. He "resided" in the back right corner of the stage and every time I talked about the Swami, I would go to that part of the stage. The result was that, after a few minutes, the back right hand of the stage was automatically associated with the Swami. The technique was so powerful that, at the end of the speech when I referred to the Swami, I just pointed to the back right hand corner of the stage and the whole audience knew who I was talking about. The effect was profound, as was clear from the comments of the gentleman who had come up to congratulate me.

Using the stage is not a common technique in public speaking, yet it can be a very powerful tool. This technique can be especially effective when there are multiple characters in a story. Great speakers are able to create multiple characters on stage, each with a different voice, physical presence, and location. Just being at a location on stage clarifies the context for the audience, letting them associate the words with a particular character. In many instances, the speaker does not even have to tell the audience who is speaking; the audience knows this by the location of the speaker on stage. The speaker can thus deliver the story knowing that the audience is not confused about the characters.

Stage use, though, is not limited to referencing characters. Here are some other examples in which the appropriate use of the stage can help clarify the words.

- When taking the audience back in time, the speaker can take a few steps back. This is a visual representation of "going back in time." Though the audience may not even notice the gesture, it reinforces the words making the impact more profound.

- Move along from one side of the stage to another when talking of events in a chronological order. If the number of events is limited, different events can be associated with different locations on stage. Just the motion in one direction, indicating the passage of time between events, is a helpful visual reinforcement for the audience.

- A common technique that falls in between gestures and stage use is the ability of a speaker to take a few steps forward toward an audience to emphasize an important point. In a one-on-one conversation, if someone leans forward to say something, the interest of the other person is immediately increased. In most cases, the person receiving the information will also lean forward in response. A similar effect takes place when a speaker moves a few steps forward toward an audience. They, too, respond with increased interest. The speaker can use this technique multiple times during a speech but should refrain from inappropriate or overuse which can dilute its effect.

Conclusions

Nonverbal communication should be considered as a secondary channel to convey information and emotion. Unfortunately, most speakers either do not use this channel or incorrectly use nonverbal communication to send messages that conflict with what they are saying. This confuses the audience.

A keen understanding of nonverbal communication techniques will help speakers even though they do not aspire to use gestures or props in their speeches. At the very least, it will make them aware of gestures they may be unconsciously using that are confusing their audiences.

For speakers who choose to reinforce their verbal messages using gestures, props, and the stage, these nonverbal communication techniques offer an opportunity to convey and reinforce emotions. When used well, nonverbal techniques can provide great impact, sometimes conveying emotions with the subtlety and clarity that words and voice alone cannot. No wonder most great speakers take the time to develop nonverbal tools and use them in their speeches on a regular basis.

Chapter 10 discusses another excellent tool to convey emotions and information: stories. This technique has been used for centuries but few understand how to develop and write them specifically for speeches. Chapter 10 is thus a must-read for all speakers.

Chapter 10

The Art of Telling a Story

Storytelling is the most powerful way to put ideas into the world today.
—Robert McKee, author and director

In the 1920s, Harvard Business School introduced the case study method to teach the business school curriculum. This method used real examples of current issues, many still unresolved, to engage students and make the subject matter interesting and memorable. This technique is now the standard teaching method in most business schools.

The case study method is an example of how a story transforms a dry topic and engages an audience. In this approach, a business scenario is presented, characters are developed, given names and personalities, and their business motivations and thought processes are revealed to the students. The students get an opportunity to see the problem through the eyes of each character, allowing feelings and emotions to be introduced into an otherwise-cerebral discussion. The case study method remains an excellent example of the use of stories as an effective tool to engage students and help them retain the subject material.

Ever since recorded history, speakers have understood the importance of stories to entertain and educate an audience. Homer's stories, created around 1200 BC, still influence modern society. Almost all people who have shaped our future throughout history, including Jesus, Buddha, and the creators of the ancient Hindu mythological texts, have been remarkable storytellers. In modern times, stories are extensively used by speakers to illustrate a point, add humor or excitement, personalize a learning event, associate with a group, or simply entertain an audience.

We can all agree that stories are commonly used by speakers but few have taken the time to consider why stories are so effective. I frequently use the following example to illustrate the reason why they are.

All of us have our favorite restaurants, the names of which are enough to make us salivate. These are the places that never tire us. In most cases, there are a couple of dishes that are just exceptional—no other restaurant makes them better. In fact, every time you go to this restaurant you order the same dish, which drives your spouse nuts because everywhere else you like to try out different things.

I want you to take a moment and imagine this favorite dish. Imagine the aroma when it is brought to the table. Imagine the first bite—the taste when it touches your tongue. Why does it feel so good? What is it about the dish that makes it special?

This exercise leads us to the following instructive questions:

- What filled your stomach, the meat or the sauce?
- What made the dish special, the meat or the sauce?

In almost all cases you will find that, though the meat and the vegetables fill your stomach, the dish is made special because of the spices and the sauce that go into it. In other words, you go to a restaurant to eat the meat but you remember it because of the sauce.

A parallel exists in public speaking and presentations. It is your story that will make the facts memorable. Just like good chefs who serve their meat with sauce and spices, good speakers tell the story behind their facts and, even though their facts may be the same as yours, the audience remembers them because of the story.

I attend many scientific presentations. The reason I choose to attend a presentation is often because of the topic being discussed. I go to get some insight on the topic, something that I may be able to apply in my area of work. However, I often find that these presentations are just a collection of facts put up on a screen. They might help advance scientific research but they are rarely memorable. Presentations would be much more enjoyable and memorable if the stories behind the research are also shared.

Why don't researchers share their stories? Time restrictions may be a primary reason. Most scientific presentations have to be finished in 20 to 30 minutes. In a short time, a researcher has to present information that she collected after many years of rigorous work. This is difficult to do.

I take a different approach to such a presentation. I do not try to capture my entire work in a short presentation but try to leave the audience with one or two memorable ideas. The interest this creates will likely result in them reading my technical paper, which is the right format to cover the entire body of research. The presentation can then include stories and other techniques that will make it memorable.

I do want to emphasize that a good story will not be enough to prop up poor research or spurious facts. An audience will be disappointed if your technical talk has no salient research points that they can learn from or apply. A good story is not a substitute for good research; it only makes the research more memorable.

Now that we know why a story is needed, let's understand how it works. In the first section of this book, we looked at the importance of emotions in making speeches memorable. A story is a perfect example of this. It allows the audience to identify with the characters in the speech so that they can feel their pain and joy. These emotions therefore make the speeches more memorable.

Where Do I Find My Story?

Many speakers believe that only life-changing events that show great adversity or momentous courage are worthy of becoming good stories in speeches. Because most of us do not have many life-changing events, this keeps many speakers from using stories in their speeches. The truth is that stories are everywhere and sometimes the most common everyday events, when looked at with a different perspective, can make the most entertaining stories. I call this perspective looking through "story glasses." Events that happen every day to you and me, such as in a grocery store or at home with our children, provide excellent material for compelling stories. The reason stories are difficult to find is that we are not looking for them—we are not wearing our story glasses. The next time you are up and around town, make sure you wear your story glasses. You will find that story-worthy incidents happen and go unnoticed all the time, only because they are not recorded, either literally or mentally.

A second step that many professional speakers take, apart from always wearing their story glasses, is always carrying an "idea pad" to record an interesting event or idea. In today's world of smart phones, a picture is an easy way to record an event. Some professional speakers prefer to make a short audio recording that captures the main points of what happened. Still others put a small pad in their pocket and record story-worthy incidents in a few words.

Most speakers eventually transfer these ideas into a story "catalogue." When transferring the story from their idea-capturing mechanism, they put down enough information about what happened so that they can recall it later. This may mean only a few words for some people or crafting the full story for others. In either case, the story is captured for future use. It will not take you very long to develop a fairly extensive database of stories that can be used when writing a speech. Speakers usually just sift through their catalogue to find an appropriate story for their speech.

Writing the Story: The Three Cs

Developing a good story from an idea requires practice and constant refinement. The story should flow and evoke emotions that are aligned with the purpose of the speech. Some writers and storytellers follow the three Cs idea to develop good stories. The three Cs stand for: character, conflict, and construction. This idea has been detailed in books on storytelling but let us explore how the emotional approach to speaking can explain why the three Cs are effective.

Character refers to the development of the characters in a story. I would be surprised if you are moved to tears when you read the obituary section of your local newspaper. The words said in memorial of the lives lost do not mean much to you. This is because you do not know the person in the memorial. Now, if you were reading the news and you suddenly find the name of a close friend, an aunt, or an office colleague, your emotional response to the memorial would be different. A speaker needs to develop his characters, particularly the main ones, such that the audience gets to know them. The better you know the character, the more emotionally attached you get to them. This makes for a much better emotional connection for the audience and a key way to succeed in delivering a good story.

Conflict is an effective tool to make a story stick. A well-developed conflict allows for thought, a place where the audience ponders and reasons. It creates emotional tension, often pitting right against wrong, creating the right environment for a strong emotional release when the conflict is resolved. A conflict is also where the audience makes the story their own because they now have opinions presented to them that they can agree or disagree with. They have to take sides, make a decision, and get emotionally involved. If the characters have been developed well, the audience feels for them as they struggle with their conflict and share in their emotional turmoil. There are few tools as effective in working with emotions as a well-developed conflict and its eventual resolution.

The third C stands for construction, which, in our case, refers to how the speech is constructed. In the approach we have discussed in this book, this most closely aligns with emotional flow. A well-constructed story will allow emotions to flow easily. The audience will not be distracted by characters they do not know or that do not belong in the story. The transitions will be smooth, allowing the audience to move seamlessly from one part of the story to the next. In short, good construction allows for the audience to follow the speaker's emotional journey.

The Structure of a Story

The story, like a speech, usually has three parts: the beginning, the body, and the ending.

The beginning. This is where the scene is set and the main characters are introduced. A good beginning will capture the attention of the audience while setting the stage for the story to flow into the body and ending. Here are a few ideas on how to engage the audience at the beginning of a story.

1. Ask a question. Often, a speaker will come to the stage and ask a question (for example, "How many of you have done...?"). This immediately engages the audience members, who have to drop all their other thoughts and concentrate on the question. It also gets them interested because they want to see how many other people in the audience are in their "camp."

2. Another commonly used approach is to make a controversial statement (for example, "Everything in life is arranged"). This technique is also very useful. Most often, the statement is controversial and the audience has a strong opinion on it. This again forces them to stop whatever they are thinking, engage, and concentrate on the statement. They might agree or disagree vehemently with it. Either way, the speaker has achieved his or her purpose.

3. Finally, the speaker may do something out of the ordinary to get the attention of the audience. One good example was illustrated by Darren LaCroix in his speech where he fell, face first, on stage. He had obviously practiced and figured out a way of doing this without hurting himself, but the audience was surprised and the "gimmick" achieved its purpose. Darren was later able to tie this gesture to the broader context of the speech. He also became the 2001 World Champion of Public Speaking.

Apart from getting the attention of the audience, the beginning sets the stage for the rest of the speech. The key characters of the speech should ideally be introduced in the beginning, even if it is just a brief mention of their names. The key characters should be allowed to develop individual personalities. There are a number of ways to bring a character to life in a story.

1. The speaker can use visual words to describe the character. This paints a picture of the character in the minds of the audience. This is similar to how authors describe their main characters in great detail, explaining their appearance, gait, voice, and accent so that the reader constructs a mental image of them.

2. The speaker uses a different voice and accent for each character. This is not always possible, but it is a powerful approach. It removes any ambiguity about which character is center stage at any moment.

3. The speaker can use different parts of the stage for different characters. This, again, has a clarifying effect for the audience so they are not confused about which character is talking or being referenced.

4. Finally, the speaker may put on a costume that portrays one of the characters. This usually works if the story is centered on

one character, with most of the speech involving him or her. It may also not be appropriate for the speaker to wear a costume, especially if the speech is being delivered in a formal setting.

Once the audience has been engaged and the characters have been introduced, the speaker is ready to move to the second part of the speech: the body.

The body. This is the main part of the story. It provides the flesh and blood to the bare-bones structure set up in the beginning. The characters are developed further and their personalities are given life. As discussed, it is important for the speaker to create a visual image of the characters for the audience. The body is also where the relationships among the characters are developed and the stage set for conflict to occur. The development of the relationships between the characters is an important aspect of making the story real. It allows for emotional connections to develop between the audience and the characters. These relationships also allow for the audience to identify themselves with the speakers.

One of the key things that happen in this part of the story is the development of a conflict. The conflict is more engaging if the alternatives offered are realistic and the conclusion of the speech is not clear. I remember while writing a speech I called "Perfect," I was struggling to make it more effective but could not identify the main reason for why it was lacking impact. The speech was filled with humor and had a good message, but was not able to deliver a strong final emotion at the end. For many weeks, I tried various options to increase the effectiveness of the speech but without success. Finally, my wife pointed out that the speech did not have a good conflict, and its impact improved dramatically once I introduced a good one in the story. You can read "Perfect" in the last chapter of this book and judge for yourself if the conflict is effective.

A conflict does not have to be a battle scene or have a bad and good side. It could be two opinions being considered. It could be an inner conflict within a character—for example, a man sitting on top of a building debating whether or not to commit suicide.

The ending. The resolution of the conflict forms the last part of a story. The resolution should answer or resolve all the questions that were raised in the beginning and the body so that the audience is not left with a feeling of uncertainty at the end. The resolution usually leaves the audience with a strong emotion. The emotion may be one of satisfaction, if the resolution is to their liking, or of anger and disgust, if they feel that justice has not been done. In every case, emotions can only form completely if all the questions have been answered and the audience gets an opportunity to form their opinion.

Typically, the speaker uses the resolution of the story to share a profound learning with the audience. This learning builds on the emotions developed as a result of the resolution of the story, and channels those emotions toward the purpose of the speech. The most common way of communicating the learning to the audience is to state it directly. Speakers can simply say, "If there is one thing that you get out of this story, let it be this..." and then proceed to lay out the main message in a few words. This approach has the advantage of clarifying the message at the end of the story so that it is not left to interpretation. The learning comes across strong and clear, making an immediate impact. This method works best for an audience that has similar backgrounds. However, this strength becomes a weakness in front of diverse audiences that have different backgrounds and draw different lessons from the same speech.

When speaking before a diverse crowd, some speakers use a different approach. They leave the audience with an open-ended, less concrete statement at the end. This allows the audience to derive the learning themselves, each member individually interpreting the speech. This type of ending is difficult to construct and requires considerable skill and practice but has the advantage of engaging a much wider audience.

Using the Story

The nature and length of the speech dictates the form in which the story is used by the speaker. A two-minute version of the story could be used in a short speech, whereas a longer keynote speech may use a 10-minute version. A speaker may also use similar stories in different speeches and draw different lessons from them on each occasion.

When the length and purpose of the speech are clear to the speaker, a suitable idea or story is selected from the speaker's story catalogue. The idea or story is then developed to its appropriate length based on the speaker's needs. The process of sculpting the story for maximum effect now begins.

A story is reviewed multiple times before it is ready. The speaker should never forget that a story works because it engages the audience at an emotional level. The speaker should identify any unnecessary parts of the story, either characters that are not essential to the context of the speech or parts of the story that do not suit the message. These should be removed. Interestingly, different characters may become important when the same story is used in a different context.

The speaker should carefully consider the flow of the story. It should develop and proceed without any abruptness. The smooth flow of a story allows for a smooth flow of thought and emotion in the audience. If at any time something unusual is presented in the story—like a new character who has not been properly introduced—the speaker will lose the connection with the audience while they try to resolve the confusion. A speaker should thus work to remove any part of the story that takes away from connecting with the audience.

I often work with speakers who have a great story and are trying to make a speech out of it. This is the wrong approach to speaking. It is like having an axe and then cutting a tree just because you have one and not because you need firewood. I constantly have to remind such speakers to not fall in love with the story—it is just a tool to convey emotions; it is not the speech itself. A story, like all other speaking tools, will lose its effectiveness if used inappropriately.

Conclusions

Stories are an integral part of a speech. They bring color and life to it, helping the speaker convey profound messages in an entertaining and enriching manner. However, it takes time to prepare a good story and even more time to practice and deliver it well. Once prepared, the same story can be used for multiple purposes by emphasizing different messages and embellishing different characters.

Many writers and speakers consider the three Cs while developing their stories: character, conflict, and construction. Character and conflict help generate emotion, and construction helps in the flow of emotions. Most stories also have a structure: the beginning, body, and ending. It helps to introduce the characters in the beginning, develop them, and then introduce the conflict in the body, resolve it, and extract the message at the end of the speech.

A good story conveys emotion, which is why it is such an effective speaking tool. PowerPoint, on the other hand, is regarded as an ineffective tool in conveying emotions. Chapter 11 goes to the heart of the problem of using PowerPoint and suggests some ideas to make effective presentations using it.

Chapter 11

Presenting With PowerPoint

Power corrupts, PowerPoint corrupts absolutely.
—Edward Tufte, professor emeritus and presentation guru

In the late 1990s and early 2000s, the Silicon Valley region in California was booming. Aspiring entrepreneurs were pitching any information technology-related idea they could get their hands on, and almost all these ideas were being funded by venture capitalists. I can imagine that Seth Godin, a marketing expert and entrepreneur, was seeing a lot of these presentations and not liking what he saw. He became so frustrated with how presenters, entrepreneurs, and executives were using PowerPoint that he wrote a short e-book on its effective use. The e-book, called *Really Bad PowerPoint*, sold for $2 on Amazon.com, became a best-seller, and is still a good reference for PowerPoint presentations.

The observation that PowerPoint is not being used properly has been noted by many communication experts. In his book *Presentation Zen*, Garr Reynolds writes: "But PowerPoint (or Keynote, etc.) is not a method; it is a tool that can be used effectively with appropriate design methods or ineffectively with inappropriate methods."

As Reynolds points out, PowerPoint slides have become synonymous with the presentation instead of being a presentation aid. Just reflect on how many times you have asked a colleague to "Send me your presentation" when you were actually asking for her PowerPoint slides. Speakers today believe that PowerPoint slides *are* their presentation, expecting fully that the audience will focus on the slides while they can proceed to merely read from them. No one is gazing at them nor can they forget the words! What could be a better way of getting rid of the speaking jitters?

In *Really Bad PowerPoint*, Seth Godin makes some interesting comments on why presenters use PowerPoint:

> The first thing that most people use PowerPoint for is a teleprompter! Think of all the presentations you've been to where the presenter actually reads the slides. Did your audience really have to come all this way to a meeting to listen to you read the slides? Why not just send them over?

> The second task is to provide a written, cover-your-ass record of what was presented. By handing out the slides after the meeting (or worse, before), the presenter is avoiding the job of writing a formal report, and is making sure that she can point to the implicit approval she earned at the meeting.

> The third task is to make it easier for your audience to remember everything you said. Sort of like reading your slides, but better. After all, if you read your slides, and then give the audience a verbatim transcript of what you read, what could be wrong with that?

Of course, having read the first section of *Emote*, you realize that this is not communication. Godin, in his e-book, points to emotion being the key ingredient that is missing in ineffective PowerPoint presentations. The copious use of text, which is accompanied by confusing design that disrupts the flow of thoughts and ideas, results in a dazed audience. No wonder Godin was suffocated by the odious discharge of incomprehensible data aimed at him and unaffected by the soulless delivery of sterile slides incapable of excitement or passion. Like Godin, I believe that we can do better.

Godin is only one of several influential communication gurus who have spoken out against poor PowerPoint slides. Another aficionado, Dr. Edward Tufte, who specializes in the visual presentation of statistical information, is particularly critical of how PowerPoint is used in companies, including technically-heavy organizations like NASA and Boeing. In his book *Beautiful Evidence*, Tufte makes his case by quoting passages from several sources. I found the following passage from the *Final Report of the Return to Flight Task Group* (July 2005), which investigated the *Challenger* disaster, particularly telling:

> We also observed that instead of concise engineering reports, decisions and their associated rationale are often contained within Microsoft PowerPoint charts or e-mails. The CAIB report (vol. 1, pp. 182 and 191) criticized the use of PowerPoint as an engineering tool, and other professional organizations have also noted the increased use of this presentation software as a substitute for technical reports and other meaningful documentation. PowerPoint (and similar products by other vendors), as a method to provide talking points and present limited data to assembled groups, has its place in the engineering community; however, these presentations should not be allowed to replace, or even supplement, formal documentation.

Godin had emphasized the first big hurdle while using PowerPoint: the loss of emotional content from the presentation. In his writing, Tufte points out the second major disadvantage with using it: PowerPoint slides have a very low bandwidth for transferring information compared to written documents. Tufte decries the use of PowerPoint as the tool of choice for documenting meetings and reports. In other words, PowerPoint slides, due to the limitations of usable text sizes and inbuilt display tools, cannot transfer dense information as effectively as other documents can. PowerPoint is thus not an ideal tool to deal with complexity in ideas, information, or data. Perhaps, a key reason for so many bad PowerPoint presentations is that presenters are trying to communicate dense and involved information using a tool not designed to communicate complexity. It is certainly a thought worth investigating.

Having read Section I of *Emote*, you realize that cluttered, complicated slides, filled with text and information, break the emotional connection of the audience with the speaker. The journey of the audience is interrupted and the speaker then spends additional time to reconnect with them. Tufte's note on the limitations of PowerPoint is partly the reason why presenters have a tough time emotionally engaging an audience while using PowerPoint slides.

If the incorrect use of the PowerPoint tool and the inability of most PowerPoint slides to engage the audience emotionally are the two main reasons responsible for a plethora of forgettable presentations, can we do something about it? On the other hand, if PowerPoint is so ineffective, why do we still use it for presentations? Should presenters move away from using PowerPoint as a presentation tool? The answer is not necessarily to give up on PowerPoint as a tool but perform a complete rethink of how we use it in presentations.

Reynolds, Godin, Tufte, and other communicators have offered many ideas on how to make effective PowerPoint slides. The objective of this chapter is not to rehash these techniques, but rather to point out one idea that will help presenters address the two reasons that are contributing to ineffective PowerPoint presentations.

To Avoid Complexity, Simplify or Slow Down

Reynolds discusses several ideas to simplify slides. Among these, the need for white space in PowerPoint slides stands out as a simple yet effective way of improving the effectiveness of a slide. He suggests that white space can imply elegance and clarity, and convey a feeling of high quality, sophistication, and importance. Nancy Duarte, an expert in presentation development and design, writes in her book *Slide:ology*: "It's okay to have clear space [in PowerPoint slides]—clutter is a failure of design."

But does this mean that presentations have to be watered down, stripping of much-needed complexity when explaining detailed, technical ideas? Having spent time at MIT, certainly among the most "geeky" places on Earth, I understand how some ideas are inherently complicated. Tufte suggests that presenters need to understand what can be achieved via a PowerPoint presentation. He recommends that serious discussions in corporations on complex, data-driven issues should involve a briefing paper or technical report that is required reading for the audience before the meeting. The content is then discussed in the meeting with the presenter, who guides the audience through the logic of the paper. The presentation can then be simple, avoiding the complexity covered in the paper but emphasizing key insights. Such a presentation can then adhere to the concept of simplicity, while still adding value.

||||||||||||||||||||||||||||||||||||||||||||||||||||||||||||||||||||||||||||||||||||||||||||||||

Simple Ideas to Improve Information Flow

Dr. Jean-luc Doumont points out that graphs shown on PowerPoint slides always have the text associated with the vertical axis rotated such that the text is written along the vertical axis from bottom going upward. There are two reasons for doing this. First, most presenters are just copying graphs from written documents, which for correct reasons, have this text rotated. Second, text rotated in this way can be written next along the vertical axis, thereby taking up less space on the slide. The presenters then can put more information on the slide. Doumont pointed out that in presentations, where clarity is paramount, this text written along the vertical axis is not reader-friendly. The audience frequently tilts their heads to be able to read the text on the vertical axis of the graph. Doumont suggests that the text of the vertical axis should either be removed and the title of the graph should convey the same information, or the text should not be rotated. This allows the audience to follow the speaker quickly, which is important for any visual on a PowerPoint slide. It also leads to more white space on the slide.

||||||||||||||||||||||||||||||||||||||||||||||||||||||||||||||||||||||||||||||||||||||||||||||||

Sometimes, especially during conference presentations, slides have to address complexity in the absence of an informed audience which has pre-read the presenter's material. In such cases, a presenter may choose to identify the one core issue that needs to be conveyed about his idea, an issue that captures the excitement about innovation for example, and then find a clear way of presenting that in a few slides. If complexity cannot be avoided, it should be introduced slowly and in a way that does not hamper the flow of thought, enabling the presenter to keep the audience engaged. For instance, complexity can be introduced slowly into a slide by either layering it with additional ones, or breaking up the original slide into multiple ones where each successive slide adds intricacy. This allows the audience to slowly absorb the material presented, making the complexity in the slides less of a hindrance. The emotions will follow once the idea is understood, making it memorable.

To Introduce Emotion, Use Visual Images and Stories

These presentation gurus (and others like them) also recommend slides being visual with few or no words. Many of these speakers use only high-resolution photographs from professional Websites, like Istockphoto.com, in their presentations. Pictures and other forms of visual stimulation engage both parts of the brain, enabling a more compelling connection of the speaker with his or her audience. The speaker can get a similar effect by using visual words that generate a picture in the minds of the audience.

Research on emotional memory may point to scientific reasons for the effectiveness of these techniques. Boston University researcher Elizabeth Kensinger, whose work on emotional memory was referenced in Chapter 3, has also looked at the response of the part of the brain called amygdala to pictures (visual stimulus) and words. Chapter 3 discussed the role of the amygdala in forming emotional memory. Using fMRI scans, Kensinger studied 21 people responding to emotional stimuli from pictures and words. The results were interesting. The fMRI scans showed that both emotional words and emotional pictures energized the left amygdala but only visual stimulus lit up the right amygdala. If the amygdala plays a critical role in emotional memory, could it be that pictures, rather than words, will be better remembered by the audience? This will certainly verify what many speakers have intuitively known for years.

Another tool that PowerPoint presenters fail to utilize is the use of stories to engage an audience. Often, presenters display only the final results but do not share the failures and tribulations in getting the data.

A few years ago, I was presenting a technical paper at an international conference. The paper was about some experiments that had been performed by our group, and the results had been rather surprising. Our team had come up with a controversial explanation, one that most researchers would not have intuitively guessed. I wanted to introduce a story into my presentation and, after some thought, decided to relate it as a Sherlock Holmes mystery case. This controversial and hugely popular character seemed a good fit. I began my presentation, like all Sherlock Holmes cases, at the crime scene, which was our lab. The data that we collected was the evidence.

Toward the end, the famous quote associated with Sherlock Holmes, "Once you have eliminated the impossible, whatever remains, however improbable, must be the truth," provided the perfect setup to introduce the controversial and unexpected hypothesis proposed to explain the experimental data. Like all Sherlock Holmes mysteries, once the crime was explained, it seemed obvious. That is how I finished my presentation.

The presentation was very well received. Several audience members came up to me afterward to say how much they enjoyed it. The use of a story in a technical presentation had set it apart. The association with the Sherlock Holmes case had brought excitement to the topic, including to those in the audience who were not familiar with the topic of the research. Everyone was trying to solve the case. Thus, both stories and pictures allow a presenter to involve the audience emotionally, making the presentations memorable.

Practical Examples

Let's look at two well-known figures and see how they are able to navigate complexity and introduce emotion into their slides. They may help in our understanding of how PowerPoint presentations can come to life.

In the early 2000s, a surprising presentation called "An Inconvenient Truth" transformed the global warming debate. This presentation finally gave voice to an issue that needed attention, showing the consequences of climate change if serious action was not taken. The presentation was surprising because its main protagonist was former vice president of the United States Al Gore, who was often called "Gore the Bore." This was also the same Al Gore who famously did not win his home state of Tennessee in the 2000 presidential election, partially because he was considered an elitist who had a lot of difficulty connecting at an emotional level with an audience. How, then, was he able to deliver a presentation that captivated the world, leading to an award-winning documentary on the issue, and resulting in Gore and others receiving the Nobel Prize? The answer, surprisingly, is in the slides.

It is clear that Al Gore did not lack passion; he just had a hard time connecting with a crowd and conveying that emotional energy to them. In the case of "An Inconvenient Truth," he found the right tools to convey that emotion. His presentation slides were almost entirely pictures. They were easy to follow and absorb. Gore stayed away from complex equations but showed visual comparisons of natural resources that have been dramatically altered due to decades of rising temperatures. These pictures, and not lines of text and equations, helped convince the audience of the scientific accuracy of the global warming phenomenon.

Surprisingly, Gore's delivery had not changed dramatically from his days in political office, but he had found a way to connect with the audience and channel his emotions. Gore's slides contrasted what was with what is to capture the horror and ravages of global warming on glaciers, providing the emotional element to his presentations. Further, his compelling story of being a man on a mission to save the world resonated with the audience, helping Gore's message become memorable. In the case of "An Inconvenient Truth," Gore used slides and a compelling story as tools to emotionally connect with the audience and take them on an emotional journey. It resulted in a great presentation.

A speaker who captured the essence of simplicity and white space in presentations was the late Steve Jobs with his iPhone launch lecture. Unlike Gore, Jobs was a charismatic speaker. He did not need slides to connect emotionally with his audience. Jobs used slides to enhance that emotional connection, keeping them very simple, elegant, and visual. In his iPhone launch speech which we referenced earlier, his 90-minute talk had more than 100 slides, less than five had more than 10 words, sometimes an entire slide was just one or two words, and almost all of them had pictures or visuals. These visuals, like pictures of the iPhone, were simple and easy to understand.

Jobs used his slides in a very different way from Gore. His slides did not convey emotionally charged content; they just allowed the emotions to flow a little better. Gore, on the other hand, used his slides as the key tool to convey emotion. His pictures, not his delivery, were the source of emotion for the audience. What is important for presenters is that both presentations used slides and were effective.

Conclusions

PowerPoint is a ubiquitous presentation tool in the modern world; most corporate presentations use it to deliver messages and information. PowerPoint is derided by many because it has led to a de-sensitization of presentations, where ill-equipped presenters hide behind slides without making even the slightest effort to connect with their audience. In general, presentations in the PowerPoint era have moved away from affecting people.

This is certainly not the fault of PowerPoint, just a lack of understanding among speakers about how to effectively use it as a tool to deliver good speeches. The inability of words and text, the most common content in slides, to effectively convey emotional information is the primary reason for the current state of affairs. In addition, presenting complex information using PowerPoint is challenging and leads to a speaker often losing his or her audience.

These challenges can be overcome if a speaker uses simple PowerPoint slides as a reinforcement tool for the main messages he or she shares with the audience. A slide with a few simple words or clear pictures and figures can be very effective in conveying emotions. If complexity cannot be avoided, then it should be introduced in stages or layers to keep the audience engaged at all times. These simple steps by a speaker will ensure an improved experience for an audience.

No discussion on speaking tools can be complete without an understanding of the cultural and personality overtones of their use. The combination of our internal wiring and past experiences, which shapes our personalities, may make some tools more suitable for a speaker. Similarly, social and cultural norms of the audience may make some speaking tools more effective than others. This understanding of how personality and culture affect the choice of the speaking tool is discussed in Chapter 12.

Chapter 12

Tools, Culture, and Personality Types

Speaking is not an act of extraversion...it is a performance,
and many performers are hugely introverted.
—Malcolm Gladwell, author, speaker, and journalist

Every year, a large percentage of the sophomore class at the Massachusetts Institute of Technology spends a week attending an experiential learning program in team performance skills. Part corporate workshop, part hands-on training, the Undergraduate Practice Opportunities Program, or UPOP, exposes MIT sophomores to the expectations and responsibilities they will encounter in the work world.

In one of the learning modules, the student group is broken into teams that are tasked with preparing a presentation for a target audience. To make the module interesting, the audience for each team has been assigned personalities based on preferred problem-solving styles: analytic (nerds), creative (space cadets), organized (bean counters), or interpersonal (touchy-feelies). The teams have to tailor their presentations to appeal to the personality type of their audience. For most of these students, this is the first presentation they have prepared keeping the needs of their audience in mind.

Professional speakers, on the other hand, never stop emphasizing the need to tailor presentations for an audience. "Research your audience" and "understand the needs of your audience" are statements commonly heard in public speaking workshops. A presentation is best, after all, when it is custom-made for the audience. But wait! If the speaker should understand the needs of his audience to deliver an effective presentation, then shouldn't he also understand his innate skills and default presentation style in order to do so? Shouldn't a speaker use speaking tools that suit her personality type to deliver effective presentations? Unfortunately, this is rarely the case. Public speaking workshops usually emphasize the same speaking tool kit for their entire class.

Susan Dunn, who is an author and trainer, writes in an article at Career-Intelligence.com that "people energize the extravert, and drain the introvert." Clearly, personality traits should influence preparation techniques. How you are wired should affect the routine you follow leading up to your presentation and who you are should dictate the tools that you employ when you speak.

There is increasing researched evidence that personality types have their origins in the brain. Debra Johnson and her colleagues report in a 1999 paper that introverts have increased blood flow in the regions that require thought, like making plans for the future, remembering events from the past, and problem solving. Does this mean that introverts will be more successful if they use words that paint visual images, or provide "aha" moments where (suddenly) concepts become clear and show how the speech affects the future of the audience? Their brains are better wired to use these tools.

In the same paper, Johnson and her colleagues found that extraverts, on the other hand, were more in the moment, getting their emotional stimulation from smell, taste, and the feelings around them. Extraverts, it seems, will revel in the traditional tools that public speakers use: large gestures, eye contact, and good motion on stage to absorb the emotion in the moment. They will get emotional when they feel the emotions of the audience and feed off them. They are more inclined to be in the moment.

Back at the UPOP module, the students are busy discussing the best approach to their presentation. As the number-one-ranked engineering school in the world for many years running, MIT is a magnet for nerds (analytic problem solvers). The kids who attend MIT are scary smart but, in the same breath that corporate recruiters sing their praises on technical know-how, they also mention the need for more team collaboration and group thinking skills. In short, this introverted bunch of students will have to learn new skills to stand out in our extraverted society.

The UPOP program was started to make the students aware of this apparent disconnect between their preferred personality traits and the expected personality traits of most of corporate America.

This bunch of uncorrupted students offers a great opportunity to observe default presentation styles for different personality types. In fact, the students themselves take a short questionnaire that identifies their preferred learning method and puts them into the same four categories as their fictitious audience: nerds, space cadets, bean counters, and touchy-feely types. Susann Luperfoy, the executive director of the UPOP program, points out that, over the last few years, more than 50 percent of the students have been self-analyzed as analytic thinkers (in the "nerd" category) and most of the remaining fall into the space cadets or bean counters. Very few fall into the touchy-feely category. In other words, most students are introverts and few are extraverts. The UPOP program thus allows for a very unique experiment—is there a default presentation tool kit for introverts? Or should the introverts put on their extravert hats when making presentations?

Luperfoy, who has been part of the UPOP program since it began in 2002, has noticed that introverts do well at the presentation modules that excite their passions. She believes that this passion can overcome any fears or hesitation they may have about their ability to present. She has also noticed that most of these students, given enough time to prepare, do fairly well on presentations. Their presentations are thoughtful, are well designed, and use logic and facts effectively to induce an emotional response from their audience. Interestingly, most of these students do not emote themselves, but rely on the idea to evoke the emotions in the audience.

What Luperfoy has noticed is well established in the research community. Introverts need time to think and digest information before they speak. They like to introspect, choose words carefully, and even get some validation from close friends before they speak in front of groups of strangers. Once they are comfortable with the material, they can deliver wonderful presentations. Indeed, Susan Dunn writes, "Extraverts speak to think. Introverts think to speak." Introverts, in other words, gravitate toward prepared speeches.

Extraverts, on the other hand, have a tendency to speak before they have thought through their speech. They like to find and resolve issues while they are delivering their presentations. In fact, they detest the hours of preparation and practice needed for a prepared speech. Impromptu presentations, in their opinion, are really their cup of tea. Extraverts, however, should remember that just because they are more comfortable in front of people does not mean that they deliver better prepared speeches.

Though an introvert will always prefer a prepared speech, sometimes things don't work that way. Opportunities to speak may come up unexpectedly. Vice presidents may ask for a two-minute summary of projects without prior notice, or an introvert may have to participate in the Table Topics section of a Toastmasters meeting. Such extemporaneous speaking opportunities may pose the most difficult presentation format for an introvert.

Despite my success in public speaking, I am an introvert. For many years, even while winning competitions using prepared speeches, I found it very challenging to excel in speaking extemporaneously on topics without prior notice or preparation. My struggles in this speaking format were greatly reduced when I realized that an extemporaneous speech does not need to be so, it just needs to look extemporaneous. Because I speak often, finding material on a wide variety of topics is not difficult. I can speak on these topics without prior notice or preparation. The only skill that I had to develop was the ability to build a bridge that relates the question that is asked of me to the stories and material that I can speak about. After some practice (and watching politicians answer questions), I realized that this is not difficult. In the event that I actually can't answer the question, I now have the confidence to simply say, "I don't know much about that, but here is what I do know..." or, "Let me get back to you on that."

This does not mean that introverts, like me, have to be disingenuous. In fact, the single biggest speaking skill that introverts bring to the podium is their genuine passion for their topic. Extemporaneous speaking requires the introvert to think and be out of his comfort zone, which disengages him from the audience and cuts off the emotional dialogue with them that is the backbone of a good speech. Introverts are better served by steering the question to topics that they are familiar with and have thought through.

Author Susan Cain is a good example of an introvert who used tools that align with her internal wiring and found success. In her book, *Quiet: The Power of Introverts in a World That Can't Stop Talking*, she writes about her struggles as a professional negotiator because her introverted style was different from the tools traditionally used and taught by other negotiators, most of whom were extraverted. It was no surprise that these tools did not fit well with Cain's personality. She ultimately developed her own style to effectively negotiate contracts, one that utilized her quiet personality, and tools, like listening and asking many questions, which were aligned with her strengths.

Influence of Culture on Choice of Speaking Tools

I was up on the podium with an 800-strong audience of men in front of me and a smaller audience of 200 women seated to my right. Saudi Arabia's conservative society did not allow the male and female attendees to sit together. I was not very surprised because many groups in India, where I grew up, would also not allow male and female worshippers to pray together in temples. While up there, I realized that the usual facial expressions that tell me how a speech is going were hidden under the women's niqab. How then can these women convey emotions without facial expressions or even eye contact with other men? Does cultural and social upbringing influence the tools that we use during verbal communication?

I asked this question of Mohammed Murad, an Egyptian who is the first Middle Eastern person to be on the executive leadership of Toastmasters International. Though Murad acknowledges that the conservative nature of these societies does put some restrictions on female speakers, he did not seem to think that veiled women in the Middle East are held back because of them. In fact, he feels that "body language and gestures are [not] avoided by any woman just because they are covered; on the contrary some are very artful and graceful in their body language and gestures." In other words, women in the more conservative parts of the Middle East have adapted and figured out culturally appropriate tools to communicate. However, if you are a speaker in the Middle East, remember that the tools that you use regularly in your country may not apply. Murad offers some advice:

> From a religious perspective, eye contact between women and men who do not have a family relationship or are very familiar with each other is kept at minimum. This is perceived as a sign of respect and keeping distance. Women are more prone to keep the eye contact away from men. Some women feel that their privacy is

being invaded when there is prolonged eye contact from men toward them. With the new generation, this is less prominent; however, women here have learned to understand the difference between prowling eye contact and a natural one.

Some other cautionary notes are found in the best-seller *Kiss, Bow or Shake Hands* by Terri Morrison and Wayne Conaway. In their book, they provide an introduction to the culture and business etiquette of many countries around the world. It is eye-opening to see how the same gestures are construed all over the world. For example, the gesture made by using the forefinger and the thumb curled into a circle, commonly used in India and the United States to signify everything is well or okay, is interpreted differently in many other countries. Colombians put this circle over their nose to indicate that a person is homosexual, and the Norwegians and Spanish consider this gesture insulting or rude. Morrison and Conaway give many other examples of etiquette and common gestures that could be interpreted in a different way in another culture. Clearly, cultural influences are important in the tools we choose to deliver our verbal messages.

Physical space and contact during conversations are also culturally sensitive. Sidney Jourard (1968) has studied the rates of touch per hour among adults from various cultures. In a coffee shop, adults in San Juan, Puerto Rico, touched 180 times per hour; those in Paris, France, touched about 110 times per hour; followed by those in Gainesville, Florida, who touched about two times per hour; and those in London, England, who touched only once per hour.

The importance of cultural nuances in verbal communication is not just for speakers who travel to international locations to deliver speeches. The global nature of corporations today has resulted in people from all cultures working together on projects. This increases the odds of managers having face-to-face communication with people from completely different cultures. Recently, one of my mentors, who also advises many other young people, confided in me that he has a hard time understanding the responses of many of his mentees of Asian origin. "They seem to agree with everything I say during the meeting but later I find out that they were completely against my suggestion," he lamented. It is obvious that cultural communication norms are affecting business communication in this case.

The answer may lie in awareness that tools to communicate messages are different around the world. If the emphasis during conversations is maintained on the emotion conveyed, an astute speaker will learn the culturally appropriate tools quickly.

Conclusions

We live in a globally connected world where interactions between people of different personalities and cultural upbringing are common. In such cases, it is unacceptable for corporations, speakers, and business professionals not to understand the implications of personality and culture on verbal communication. Such ignorance could lead to expensive mistakes, but even worse than that, an inability to connect with groups of people of a certain personality or cultural heritage.

On the flip side, this understanding brings immense versatility and power to an experienced speaker. The awareness to look for feedback in the form of emotional undercurrents when dealing with different personalities and in different cultures, and the ability to process these messages and change the communication using this feedback is a sure way to distinguish a speaker from others. In most cases, it is a necessary skill for a successful global leader.

As with many other skills, excellence in speaking will provide benefits in other, and sometimes unexpected, ways. Section III discusses two important areas that benefit from improved communication skills: emotional intelligence and good listening skills.

Part III

Other Benefits of Good Communication Skills

Chapter 13

Emotional Intelligence

*Emotional intelligence emerges as a much stronger predictor
of who will be most successful, because it is how we handle
ourselves in our relationships that determines
how well we do once we are in a given job.*
—Daniel Goleman

"It can get very intense," the instructor said. "Some people may feel like crying, others may laugh. Do not be distracted. Be with yourself. Feel your emotions."

These were the words uttered by the instructor of the flagship course of the Art of Living Foundation. I had signed up to learn a unique breathing routine called the Sudarshan Kriya developed by Sri Sri Ravi Shankar, the founder of the organization. I was eager to get started and curious how a simple breathing routine could provide an intense experience.

The Sudarshan Kriya, Sri Sri Ravi Shankar's gift to humanity, is based on a simple premise. If a particular emotion can be associated with a breathing pattern, then forcing the same breathing pattern could trigger that emotion. This opens up the possibility to perform controlled breathing exercises to completely change a person's emotional state. Sri Sri, as he is often called, devised the Sudarshan Kriya, a set of breathing exercises that puts people in an elevated emotional state. He recommends doing a shortened version of the Kriya every day and then the "long Kriya" with a group of people including a trained expert. I was about to perform the longer version of the Kriya.

The Kriya began slowly but quickly picked up steam. As the breathing became intense, so did the emotions. I remember thinking in the middle of it that maybe I should stop; there was too much energy inside of me. At the end, a period of rest followed. I did hear people laugh or cry. I did neither, maybe because the introvert in me would not have been comfortable doing either. I remember the distinct feeling that I never knew that I had so much energy in me. It was a revelation.

The second revelation for me was the validation of Sri Sri Ravi Shankar's basic premise—that controlling breath can control emotions. In many ways, Sri Sri was using a symptom, the breathing pattern, to cure the problem, emotions. This approach is particularly attractive because breathing is natural to us, something we do anyway. Hence practicing the routine required learning no new skills, it just required learning some controlled breathing exercises. This was a powerful method.

Just like a particular breathing pattern was one of the indicators of an associated emotion, effective communication skills are an indicator of emotionally intelligent leaders. Cary Cherniss and Daniel Goleman write in the book *The Emotionally Intelligent Workplace*:

> Creating an atmosphere of openness with clear lines of communication is a key factor in organizational success. People who exhibit the communication competence are effective in the give-and-take of emotional information, deal with difficult issues straightforwardly, listen well and welcome sharing information fully, and foster open communication and stay receptive to bad news as well as good. This competence builds on both managing one's own emotions and empathy; a healthy dialogue depends on being attuned to others' emotional states and controlling the impulse to respond in ways that might sour the emotional climate. Data on managers and executives show that the better people can execute this competence, the more others prefer to deal with them.

Goleman indicates that there are certain components of emotional intelligence (EI) that facilitate effective communication. Could it be that building effective communication skills using an emotion-based approach can help build some components of emotional intelligence? I venture to guess that many will agree with this statement except that, until now, a comprehensive emotion-based method to verbal communication has not been proposed. I hope this book fills that gap.

Like the Sudarshan Kriya, this idea is attractive because presentations and other forms of verbal communication are ubiquitous in the modern workplace. Conversation and exchange of ideas are being further encouraged, for good or bad, by corporations moving to the open floor plan office concept with cubicles and no rooms. Presentation and communication provide a training opportunity for employers in the normal course of business. The employees need only understand the fundamentals of an emotion-based verbal communications approach. Awareness of how emotions can be used to craft extraordinary presentations using the concepts of final emotion, initial emotions, and the emotional journey will help employees develop key components of emotional intelligence. Is it possible, then, that building effective verbal communication skills can help provide an emotionally intelligent workplace?

Before we study how an emotion-based communication method can help build emotional intelligence, let's understand the basics of EI.

What Is Emotional Intelligence?

The book *Emotional Intelligence* shattered the basic premise of corporate recruitment and success. Until then, human resources considered IQ as the key parameter that governed potential success in an organization and recruited accordingly. However, Goleman in his 1995 book proposed that a minimum IQ was indeed required for success but, beyond this threshold IQ level, corporate success was much better tracked by EQ, or emotional quotient. Over the next few years, corporations scrambled to adapt to this changed work world, introducing EQ measurements as part of the recruitment process, identifying high-potential managers using EQ tests, and including EQ training for middle and upper management.

Researchers now believe that people are born wired a certain way. However, what happens to this wiring depends on the environment. The brain is plastic and shows immense ability to strengthen these wirings based on exposure and experience. Researchers also found subtle differences between the EI of males and females. For example, women are more able to be in the moment and be aware of emotions as they occur. Men, on the other hand, are better able to deal with stressful and corrosive emotions. However, no correlation has been found between personality types and EI, indicating that introverted and extraverted populations have the same average EI. Further, these traits can be learned and EI generally increases with age.

The Four Components of Emotional Intelligence

Seminal work, by Daniel Goleman and Richard Boyatzis among others, identified traits that were common in people who were successful in the corporate environment. These traits could be collected in four broad headings, called the four components of emotional intelligence: self-awareness, self-management, social awareness, and relationship management. Self-awareness and self-management are about personal competence, whereas social awareness and relationship management are indicators of the social competence of a person. Let's understand each one of these components before investigating how verbal communication training can help build EI.

Self-awareness. The foundational skill for personal competence is self-awareness. A self-aware leader is in synchrony with his emotions, moods, and drives. He understands his strengths and weaknesses, and has a realistic outlook on his abilities. Self-aware people exhibit self-confidence and are not afraid to make fun of themselves.

Self-awareness is also a strong indicator of success in a corporate environment. Using survey results from more than 500,000 people, Travis Bradberry and Jean Greaves report in their book *Emotional Intelligence 2.0* that 83 percent of those who scored high in self-awareness were top performers and only 2 percent of bottom performers had high self-awareness. Similarly, Goleman found from 360-degree competence assessments that people with high self-awareness rarely overestimate their strengths, something that was commonly seen in others with lower self-awareness.

Developing self-awareness requires introspection and an honest discussion with the self. Bradberry and Greaves provide 15 strategies to improve self-awareness. Most, like "Feel Your Emotions Physically," are introspective in nature. A few, like "Seek Feedback," require interaction with others.

Self-management. Self-management, the second part of personal competence, is to understand and control how emotions are affecting judgment and actions. It is characterized by the ability of a person to regulate his or her moods and emotions, to refrain from emotion-driven action and to suspend judgment until emotions have dissipated. This component of EI enables a person to step back from an emotionally charged atmosphere and ask, "Why is this happening and how can I influence it?"

Examples of self-management could be taking action even in the face of fear or being able to productively work with incompetent or unprofessional coworkers. Naturally, this competence is greatly enhanced if a person is self-aware. People with high self-management skills are comfortable with ambiguity and embrace change. They are perceived as trustworthy and having high integrity.

Preparation helps improve self-management, improving the odds that emotions will not lead to an inappropriate action. Taking time before acting, especially during emotional times, is also useful. Self-talk or discussions with trusted friends are also ways to improve self-management skills.

Social awareness. Social awareness is the ability recognize the emotions of others and adjust the message based on their emotional response. This emotional feedback system forms the backbone of socially aware leaders. This competence requires keen emotional awareness, being in the moment, deep understanding of emotional drivers, and empathy.

Socially aware people are known for their service to clients and customers. They usually perform well in cross-cultural situations and are good at recruiting and retaining talent.

Social awareness is increased primarily by listening. Actively observing nonverbal emotional carriers like voice, tone, gestures, and facial expressions can lead to increased social awareness.

Relationship management. The forth component of EI is relationship management. This refers to the ability of leaders to build lasting relationships and find common ground that allows solutions to blossom and work to progress. Relationship management skills are truly a culmination of all the other three traits. The best way to build this component is to build the other three components.

Building EI in Corporations

Considering the high correlation between leadership in the corporate sector and EI, coupled with the research that EI can be increased, it is no surprise that businesses expend considerable resources to help mid- and top-level managers increase their EI. These courses first measure emotional intelligence using a 360-degree feedback or a set of questions specifically designed to measure skill in each component of EI. Once deficiencies have been identified, specific coaching is provided to eliminate gaps in EI.

Though there are advantages for leaders to attend these courses, even if it only increases EQ awareness, it limits the training to only a few "high-potential" individuals and only when they are many years into their careers. A vast majority of corporate employees are never exposed to the benefits of EI. They never get guidance on methods to enhance their EI. This is obviously sub-optimal.

Now consider using an emotion-based communication program, among other techniques, to improve the EI of employees. For one, the approach is not elitist but targets the development of an organization's emotional quotient at the ground floor. Second, since presentations and verbal communication are activities that all employees at all levels of the corporation do on a regular basis, they provide an ideal training platform to develop EI. It would not require special settings or courses to practice activities that take the workforce away from productive activity. With the number of presentations that commonly occur in the corporate environment, there will be no shortage of forums to practice an emotion-based verbal communication approach leading, at a minimum, to an emotionally aware workforce. Improvements in verbal communication will indirectly help enhance the average EI of the workplace, leading to more productivity and better results. The icing on the cake is that a corporation has to make a minimum investment to reap the benefits that will follow. It is truly a win-win situation.

Advantages of High EI in Social Settings

The increase in EI is also beneficial in social settings because it requires speakers to look within and understand their emotions. In Section I, I gave an example of developing speech ideas based on emotional awareness. This approach emphasizes the need for a speaker to be aware of her emotions and ask why she does get emotional. When a particular scene from a movie gets me emotional, I pause and wonder how the director created the scene. I wonder how the music contributed to the enhancement of those emotions. I reflect on how the script, gestures, and facial expressions of the actors contributed to my emotional response. I do this because, often, I like the emotion I am feeling and I would like my audience to feel the same way. In that case, I can learn from the tools used in the movie to recreate the emotion.

This awareness of one's emotion is the hallmark of the self-awareness component of an emotionally intelligent person. The approach to communication helps develop this awareness, which can then be used in all aspects of communication.

Finding the Final Emotion: An Exercise in Self-Awareness

The day I won the semi-final of the World Championship of Public Speaking, it really did not sink in. After the contest, I was too tired to think about the next day; the final was six weeks away. A short two-week trip to India followed and, when I settled back in my apartment just outside of Boston, I had four weeks to write the most important speech of my life.

I had no idea what the speech was going to be about. I had no half-developed stories and no ideas that I was working on. The speech had to start from scratch. What I did have was a process of writing speeches, developed over a few years of competitive speaking. I sat down in my 700-square foot apartment and closed my eyes, trying to stay true to the technique I had developed. I focused on an emotion that I had experienced in the past, trying to revive a feeling so powerful that it would shake me to the core. I was searching for my final emotion.

The answer did not come easily. I pondered for hours, going back many years in search of strong emotional events. Many feelings came to mind, but they were covered in multiple layers of analysis and reflection. They were not pure. After a week of introspection, I finally had the emotions that I wanted to convey to my audience. I then put those feelings into words.

The emotions I uncovered were based on a sinking feeling I have during times when I question the very purpose of my life. The panic I feel when I realize I may not know my purpose; that I have "wasted" so many years; the shudder I feel that I may not be living my life, followed by the realization that I do not even know why I exist. In short, the feeling best captured by the question "Who am I?"

I wanted my audience to feel that emotion and I wanted it to be so strong that they would be forced to look deep within themselves to find the answer. That was going to be my final emotion.

You may have already noticed that the process I used to determine the final emotion is very similar to what researchers and EI gurus ask business executives to do to develop self-awareness. The understanding of the self, emotions, and their effect on action is one way of determining the final emotion. It is also an effective way to build self-awareness.

Earlier chapters have discussed how the preparation for a presentation begins when the final emotion is defined. This exercise of determining the final emotion should be carried out by presenters every time they speak. In many cases, it is determined by the purpose of the talk. In such cases, it could take only a few minutes to determine the final emotion. Understanding the emotions of the audience at the end of the speech should lead to a high-quality presentation. It will also lead to increased self-awareness.

Writing and Delivering a Speech: An Exercise in Self-Management and Social Awareness

The process of writing and preparing a speech requires the speaker to understand the emotions being evoked in the audience. During the speech, a good speaker is in the moment, continually changing the speech in subtle ways based on the emotional feedback being received from the audience. After the speech, the speaker can request specific feedback from the audience members that focuses on how they felt during and at the end of the speech. This allows him to compare his perception of the emotions being evoked to the actual feelings that the audience felt, a test of the speaker's social awareness skills.

This feedback allows the speaker to make changes to the speech to address discrepancies between the desired emotions and the evoked emotions. The feedback also puts a mirror in front of the speaker, checking his or her ability to gauge the emotions of the audience in real time. Effective speakers have a highly developed ability to gauge the emotions of the audience and make changes during the speech. This ability allows them to deliver great presentations in front of diverse groups and personality types, in different cultural settings and environments. This skill is similar to the self-management component of EI.

Effective speakers understand how their speeches are affecting their audiences and, according to EI experts, effective leaders have the same skill.

An Effective Communicator: Building Relationship Management Skills Through Communication

Being an effective communicator requires awareness far beyond the time spent during a conversation or speech. Good communicators will pick up emotional cues during coffee conversations, nonverbal behavior, and the general mood of people around them. They will notice both the crowd and the speakers before they go up on stage, feel the enthusiasm or anticipation before their presentations, and be keenly aware of the important stakeholders and their positions on the topics being addressed in their presentations. These abilities are the basics of the relationship management component of EI.

Dana Lamon, the professional speaker I mentioned earlier who is blind, provides an excellent demonstration of these skills in a public speaking environment. Lamon has developed a heightened sense of awareness for audience emotion, which allows him to be a more effective speaker. When I asked him how he does it, he sent me this reply:

> I arrive at a venue early to listen to the crowd in informal settings, such as break between sessions. I listen for enthusiasm, chattiness, laughter, and volume. This tells me about the willingness and ease of expressing feelings. I can feel if the audience is warm or not, which tells me how receptive they will be to my message.
>
> I prefer not being the first speaker to a group that is new to me. I like observing the group's reaction to other speakers; particularly speakers from within the organization. This tells me how they feel about the organization and/or the organization's leaders. I also can learn if they will be receptive to an outsider.
>
> The responses, applause, laughter, and other audible interjections mentioned above for orientation, also let me know if my audience is with me, if they are following me, and how they are connecting emotionally with me.

Lamon has been able to develop strong relationship management skills because his profession as a public speaker requires that awareness. Practice and feedback have allowed him to reinforce his innate wiring and make it stronger in this respect. I should note that Lamon is not an expert in EI. Along with his answer, he also sent me a note thanking me for asking these questions because it allowed him to introspect and figure out how he was able to work with emotions while speaking. Lamon had developed an expertise in the relationship management component of EI in the process of developing himself as a professional speaker.

Conclusions

Many components of EI can be developed while performing tasks that force individuals to work with emotions. A successful method should include activities that build EI in the process of day-to-day work. This is where an emotion-based approach to speaking can be useful.

The approach to speaking introduced in this book requires considerable introspection and awareness of personal emotions. Further, it requires a speaker to understand the sources of those emotions, and develop the ability to feel them in others. An effective speaker is not only able to communicate the emotions he is feeling, but also understands those evoked in his audience and changes his speech based on that feedback. Finally, a good communicator goes beyond the realm of communication and gathers valuable information through nonverbal emotional cues from the people and environment around her.

These skills developed in becoming a good verbal communicator will automatically develop strengths in various EI components. If taken to heart by an organization, this can lead to a more emotionally intelligent workplace. The repercussions to developing effective verbal communication skills go far beyond communication. They lead to an intelligent and productive workforce.

Chapter 14

Developing Listening Skills

Seek first to understand, then to be understood.
—Stephen R. Covey

In a *Businessweek* article called "Why Leadership Means Listening" (January 31, 2007), Carmine Gallo, author and former reporter, writes a story about a meeting between his reporter friend and former U.S. President Bill Clinton:

> [T]his reporter told me he had met Clinton after the former president gave a speech in South Africa. According to the reporter, "Clinton looked me in the eyes and seemed to have a genuine interest in what I was saying. His gaze never left me. He made me feel like the most important person in the room at the time, and Microsoft founder Bill Gates was standing right next to us!"

Good listening skills, as this reporter found out, are an integral part of verbal communication. It is a quality that often separates truly effective communicators from just eloquent orators. Given its importance, one would expect listening to be a skill commonly found among C-suite leaders. It turns out, surprisingly, that this is not the case. Executive Coach

Ram Charan writes in *The Harvard Business Review Blog* (June 2012) that his observation and analysis of many 360-degree feedback sessions shows that one in four CEOs has a listening deficit. In the 2012 edition of the *McKinsey Quarterly*, then Amgen CEO Kevin Sharer says he was a poor listener for most of his career and only learned to listen well toward the end of it. These examples should make you stop and take notice. It is indeed rare to find effective listeners.

Our listening deficit starts when we are young. Studies have shown that 70 to 80 percent of life is spent communicating. Of this time, 45 percent is listening, 30 percent is speaking, 16 percent is reading, and 9 percent is writing (Nichols, 1962). Other studies show that more than 50 percent of the time in schools is spent listening, followed by speaking, reading, and writing. Isn't it strange then that the distribution of the amount of training given, both in school and in corporate settings, is in the reverse order? We spend years training to write better and almost no time learning to listen. Sadly, we just assume that listening skills are inherent because we have been hearing since birth. Hearing and listening are completely different.

It can be difficult to appreciate good listening skills until you have experienced it yourself. I have had opportunities to witness acts of good listening at Toastmasters clubs. Toastmasters International knows a thing or two about the important elements of public speaking. The organization has championed the need for better speakers since 1925, and listening plays a critical role in the organization's main forum to build better communicators—the weekly club meeting.

A typical Toastmasters club meeting is comprised of three main elements: prepared speeches, impromptu speaking (they call it Table Topics), and a feedback session. All sessions build listening skills, but the feedback session in particular is designed to help people listen and provide effective feedback. During feedback sessions, good listeners stand out. They provide precise critiques without repeating the speech back to the speaker and share their understanding of the key elements of the speech. They point out specific sections in the speech that need improvement, recalling gestures and vocal intonations that can be made more effective by the speaker. For every area of improvement, they suggest a remedy for the speaker. I have personally received feedback on a number of occasions that left me dumbfounded by its depth of perception and detailed observation of nonverbal cues.

Do you get effective feedback after presentations or during your job performance review? Is it filled with generalities with no specific, actionable guidance provided to the speaker? I would not be surprised if it is.

Why Are We Bad Listeners?

Imagine playing this game. A puzzle is delivered to you every five minutes. It takes you about two minutes to solve the puzzle. Then you have nothing to do for the next three minutes before the next one arrives. After solving a few, you will become aware of the excessive time between them. You will start to come up with ideas on how to productively spend the three minutes of waiting time between solving a puzzle and receiving the next one. You may start planning the party you are throwing next week, or a trip you are planning. You may even try to get some reading done. In every case, you will try to "fill" the "wasted" time with more "useful" activities.

Did you realize that this game simulates what happens when you listen? Research has shown that our brains can comprehend words at a much faster rate than we can speak. Typical speaking rates range from 120 words to 180 words per minute. Researchers have found that individuals can understand words without loss of comprehension even if they were spoken at three times that speed. These results have been confirmed by various groups, some claiming even faster rates of comprehension. Our brains, thus, have a lot of "free" time when we listen. What do you think we do with this free time? As with our example game, we have a tendency to "fill" in this time with other, more "useful" activities. It turns out that this is one of the root causes of our poor listening skills.

The useful activities that fill this free time may include thinking about what needs to be done next, trying to resolve problems at home or work, working up lunch plans, and so on. Even though the individuals think they are just filling in the free time while listening, this daydreaming gets in the way of listening.

In our game, the puzzles were delivered every five minutes. What would happen if one of them came in a little early, say after four minutes and 30 seconds? You would probably be caught off-guard and possibly not be ready to hear the instructions. This could lead to you not being able to solve the puzzle. A similar scenario usually occurs with speaking. The audience is often thinking about other things during the speech and misses the words or ideas of the speaker. This is the essence of poor listening.

The second reason for poor listening skills is that people listen to respond. If the audience members try to evaluate the speaker during a conversation, they are thinking of counter arguments, shooting holes in the speaker's logic, preparing their retort, or are stuck on emotional words that were used by the speaker. Listening in order to respond makes the audience engrossed in arguments within themselves; it's all about them. They lose the ability to observe the nonverbal signals being communicated by the speaker. They sometimes stop hearing the speaker completely because they are focused on the internal dialogue taking place within their heads. Listening to respond greatly reduces the efficiency of listening.

Do All Good Listeners Listen the Same Way?

Research has shown that people fall between two extremes when it comes to listening. On one end are those who are linear listeners. They can follow a speaker from point A to point B without the need for active listening. These passive listeners are wired in such a way that they tend to have better listening skills. On the other end are the associative listeners. These listeners understand by associating the words to things they already know. They have to be constantly thinking and associating to be able to follow the speaker.

Every good listener will be naturally wired to listen a certain way. This default listening style will likely be somewhere in the middle of the two extremes. Some listening might happen by association but, on other occasions, listening may be linear.

Improving Your listening: Level 1 Listening

If listening is critical, how then can we increase our effectiveness as listeners? I believe that improving listening skills requires a fundamental understanding of the act itself. Some clues are found in a study conducted many decades ago by Ralph Nichols where he identified the key traits of good and bad listeners ("The Ten Bad Listening Habits of Americans"). Hidden in his paper is an important difference between good and bad listeners. Nichols found that good listeners were trying to get the overall idea of the speaker and not concentrating on the facts. They were not worrying about each word and each number, but were absorbing all the signals being communicated by the speaker to form a picture of what he or she was trying to say. Other research on good listening habits supports the findings of Nichols that good listeners—sometimes called Level 1 listeners—understand and respect the message being put across by the speaker. They not only hear the words and interpret them, but also receive and digest a host of nonverbal cues being communicated by the speaker.

The key to better listening skills, it seems, comes down to two things. First is the ability to absorb nonverbal messages and integrate them with the words. This allows the listener to form a comprehensive understanding of the message being communicated. This requires listeners to use the time they have while listening to not only comprehend the words but also to understand the nonverbal signals and the emotions of the speaker. This also allows them to stay focused on the speaker and prevents their minds from wandering.

The second key to better listening skills is to practice active listening. This approach achieves the same purpose. It fills in time between comprehension and delivery by keeping the listener engaged. People who practice active listening constantly ask questions like "Did this example make sense?" or "Was this story relevant?" or "What is he trying to say?" Further, they sometimes summarize the key points of the speaker in their heads to enhance memory. This form of listening forces the listener to devote his or her full attention to the speaker, reducing the chances of being side-tracked with irrelevant issues.

You may be wondering why I am emphasizing listening in a book on verbal communication. You've already realized that good listening is an essential part of communication. Further, however, effective verbal communication using an emotional approach develops many of the skills that are needed to become an effective listener. Now that we understand what good listening requires of us, let's see how the approach to communication presented in this book builds listening skills.

Developing Listening Skills Using Emotions

Consider an effective speaker who understands that a speech is really an emotional dialogue with the audience. The speaker conveys his or her emotions to the audience using various speaking tools. The speech evokes emotions in the audience. These emotions are then mirrored by the speaker as he or she "feels" them. This ongoing feedback loop is the core of a good speech. By now you realize that this feedback loop is also the key strength of good listeners, enabling them to get an overall picture of what the speaker is saying.

Intuitively, this would make sense. A speaker, who is attuned to listening to the emotional feedback of his or her audience, will likely pick up nonverbal cues during conversations. During a discussion, he or she will understand the message being conveyed by others and not just listen to their words. Thus, the speaker will be able to compile a more complete picture of the conversation, leading to better comprehension of the point of view of other participants in the discussion.

What may not be intuitively clear is that this process fills up the "free" time due to the difference between rate of comprehension and rate of delivery. The lack of free time lends itself to captivated and engaged attention without a listener forcing himself to listen. This "understand to comprehend" approach was what former Amgen CEO Kevin Sharer discovered in the later years of his career. Sharer realized that being an effective listener requires listening to many nonverbal signals to understand the motivations of the speaker. This same understanding helps a speaker deliver a great speech. Good verbal communication skills truly build good listening habits.

Sharer's epiphany on listening also brings out another habit that good verbal communicators have: they are in the moment. Sharer was forced to be in the moment, aware of the words and emotions of the speaker, understanding and absorbing the nonverbal dialogue in the conversation. In Section I, we discussed the importance of a good speaker to always be in the moment, engaging in a back-and-forth of emotions with his or her audience. This is the only way a speaker can feel the emotions. In Section II, we also emphasized how poor speakers get lost in the words and lose the connection with the audience. Sharer's experience shows us that good listeners also have the ability to stay in the moment. This critical skill is required in verbal communication and listening.

Receiving Feedback: An Exercise in Active Listening

In addition to delivering speeches while being aware of the emotional feedback of the audience, another great way to develop listening skills is to give and receive feedback. Here we discuss how receiving feedback can improve listening skills.

Receiving feedback can be confusing and, on many occasions, contradictory to expectations. As a speaker, I have delivered speeches only to receive criticism suggesting changes to parts of my speech that were considered excellent the previous day by a different person. On other occasions, I have received feedback from my manager about a particular area that needs development that I, and many others who know me well, consider to be one of my greatest strengths. Understanding and deciphering feedback requires good listening skills.

While receiving feedback on speeches, I have found that many people who provide it are not always able to articulate clearly the issue that is causing them concern. They feel that something is not right but have a hard time pinpointing the problem. As a speaker, I frequently refrain from taking the words at face value and go deeper to understand the feeling being communicated by the criticism. Why is the person uncomfortable with the speech? What is the feeling that is causing him or her discomfort? These questions lead me to the essence of the feedback.

This exercise is a classic example of active listening. The speaker is listening to understand the problem with his speech, not defend his speech. By constantly asking herself questions to enable better comprehension, the speaker can understand the true objection of the evaluator. The speaker may also summarize the main points brought up by the evaluator, either in his mind or after the evaluation, to make sure his comprehension of the issue is aligned with what the evaluator was saying. This is the essence of active listening.

Be in the Moment: A Mind Free of Thought

We are so programmed to do something all the time that our minds cannot be doing "nothing." Our minds are constantly thinking, calculating, computing, or dreaming. They are just never still. We have trained them never to stay still. This is one reason why we are poor listeners; our minds have to fill in any spare time with another activity. Can we learn to keep our minds still? Can we be taught to do nothing for a period of time?

The answer lies with the Art of Living Foundation, the group that gave this world the Sudarshan Kriya. The Art of Living Foundation practices a particular type of meditation called Sahaj Samadhi (loosely translated to mean "easy meditation"). The idea is to have the mind be completely free of thought for 20 minutes. This exercise, as I found out, is incredibly difficult. I had trained my mind to always be on the go. Our society today, particularly in the Western countries, has associated success with "doing." Taking a breather is considered a sign of weakness; doing nothing is not acceptable. Keeping thoughts out of my mind, doing nothing, turned out to be very hard. With practice, I got better and felt the benefits of Sahaj Samadhi.

Sahaj Samadhi teaches us to be in the moment. A mind free of thought is aware of all the senses. It is able to appreciate the beauty of what is around us and is able to listen. When we listen to a talk, presentation, or a conversation, a hundred different ideas flood our mind. Because we cannot keep our minds free of thought, we are busy "doing" things in our minds between the words. We are never fully in the moment listening. Sahaj Samadhi and other similar techniques are ways of breaking that vicious cycle, of learning to be in the moment. A mind able to free itself of thought, if only for a few minutes, is better able to absorb the nonverbal signals of communication. The ability to be in the moment leads to better listening skills.

Some of the ideas discussed in Section I implicitly require being in the moment. This should not be surprising because I have repeatedly emphasized in this book that doing so is a key to better verbal communication. Our emotions and those of the audience are felt only by being in the moment. For example, Section I discussed the process of identifying the final emotion in a speech. This process calls for introspection and, in many cases, it requires a speaker to slow down and feel the emotions inside of him or her. When listening to yourself, hearing your inner voice, not doing anything but just feeling, the ability to be in the moment is critical. If we only provide the same kind of attention to conversations that happen outside, we would be great listeners. And we can. The same process of quieting the mind to hear within is helpful in listening to external communication.

Conclusions

Good listening skills are an essential part of communication and are particularly important in the current global business and social environment. The fact that words don't always mean the same in all cultures and that people sometimes use the wrong words (especially when speaking or writing in a second language), emphasizes the need for listening to comprehend. By developing active listening skills and by absorbing nonverbal cues, the listener can get to the real meaning of what is being said. This is only possible if the listener goes deeper than the words.

A speaker who works with the emotions of an audience develops the ability to feel emotions and understand nonverbal cues. Further, the act of receiving feedback develops active listening, because it allows the speaker to understand the key reason behind the issues raised by the evaluator. In many cases, the key issue is the same across many evaluations, even though they are being put across in different ways and using dissimilar examples.

The ability to listen continues to be a rare trait. An effective verbal communicator develops good listening skills as he or she develops into a good communicator. For others, learning to listen continues to require additional effort and personal motivation.

Chapter 15

Putting It All Together

You've been asked to speak at a dinner gala. This is a big occasion, with a few hundred people attending. The who's who of your community will be there, flouting their latest dinner wear and elegant suits. There will be good food, an entertaining Master of Ceremonies and, of course, you.

After the initial surprise and excitement following the request, the magnitude of the task at hand has begun to sink in. The gala is a fundraiser for a nonprofit organization called Adarsh, which works for underprivileged children in underdeveloped countries. Adarsh helps fund their schooling, fulfill their basic needs of food, shelter, and clothing, and provides them an opportunity to move out of the deplorable conditions that surround them. You believe deeply in the cause and have donated generously to Adarsh in the past. You immediately realize that this is not just an everyday speaking opportunity. This is an occasion to make a difference, to be acknowledged by the community leaders, and to stand out and be noticed. As you think more and more about the speech, however, fear begins to set in.

Luckily, you have just finished reading *Emote*, which introduces a unique emotion-based approach to writing and delivering a speech. You were fascinated by the method and think that preparing your speech for the gala is the perfect opportunity to put it into practice. You have strong emotions for the cause and if the author's approach allows you to tap into that emotional energy and share it with your audience, you are certain it will impact them in a profound way. You are beginning to see how the right emotions conveyed effectively could make a difference in the lives of the people who attend the gala. The audience would feel the plight of these underprivileged children and understand what they go through on a daily basis just to survive. You feel certain that such strong emotions would encourage your community members to open their wallets and contribute to help the organization achieve its goals.

You visualize yourself delivering the speech. Midway through it, you can see that the audience has been visibly moved by your words. Some have been brought to tears; others are holding back their emotions. At the end of the speech, you also notice a glow on the faces in the audience, as if they have been inspired to make a difference and motivated by a cause greater than themselves. As these images flash through your mind, you think, "Wow! Wouldn't it be great to deliver a speech like this?" You are certain this is a perfect time to try out the ideas discussed in *Emote*.

You go back and review the ideas discussed in the book. You realize that one of the first things you should do is come up with the final emotion that you want to leave the audience with. Then you wonder: "How do I develop this final emotion?" You read Chapter 4 of *Emote* again.

As you read this chapter, you realize that developing this final emotion requires an understanding of what you would like your audience to do and think after hearing your speech. "This is more concrete," you think. You could get started on this. But all the reviewing and reading has made you tired. You plan to start on the speech tomorrow.

The next day, you sit down in a quiet place after breakfast and begin thinking about the purpose of the speech. Clearly, you would like the community to contribute to the cause. It is a fundraiser, after all, and the organizers will expect your keynote to result in more funds being generated for the organization. This has to be a key purpose of the speech.

But you want your keynote to do more. Our lives are so busy these days that not many would like a rah-rah motivating speech on a Friday evening. You think that providing your audience with a good time in a relaxed setting would be well received after a hard week in the office. You want them to feel they made a good decision by attending the gala. You also feel that this ties in well with your first objective. Attendees are likely to be more generous if they are in a relaxed mood and having fun.

Finally, you are keenly aware that having vision and leaving a legacy are concepts that will play well with your audience. You want to address them in your keynote. You believe that these concepts will not only inspire your audience but also help them better appreciate the work being done by the organization. You want the audience to be inspired by these children, to see the strength displayed by them, and be motivated to do courageous things in their own lives. Your mind wanders as you remember the story of a child laborer who was made to work 16 hours every day in inhumane conditions for almost no wages. He is free today and getting an education because of this organization. This would make an excellent story for your speech. You bring your mind back to the task at hand and remember that Chapter 9 in *Emote* cautions against writing speeches around stories and, instead, to use the right story for the speech. You force yourself back to developing the purpose of the speech.

You summarize the key objectives of your speech:

- Community contributes money.
- Community members take on initiatives in their everyday lives.
- Community has a good time.

You reflect on these objectives for your speech. They are ambitious but represent what you want to achieve with your keynote. You think you are in a position now to develop the final emotion you've learned about in *Emote*. You close your eyes and think about which emotions would lead you to contribute money to an organization. After some thought, you decide:

   a. You would contribute if you feel there is a genuine need (emotion: empathy, sympathy).

   b. You would contribute if you feel that your funds can make a real difference (emotion: empowering, excitement).

This exercise provides you with an understanding of the desired emotional state of the audience that would encourage them to fulfill your first objective. Your second objective is that the community is inspired. Again, you close your eyes and imagine how you would feel when you are inspired:

a. You would take on more initiatives in your daily life if you are inspired by children beating great odds to succeed (emotion: inspired, empowered).

b. You would take on more initiatives in your daily life if you see that these actions help you leave a legacy of men and women reaching out and helping others in spite of their limitations and hurdles (emotion: inspired).

Finally, you would like the audience to have some fun. You think about how you feel when you are having fun:

a. You think you have the most fun when no one is judging you or expecting something from you. You feel relaxed when you are having fun (emotion: sense of belonging, comfort).

b. You have fun when you are engaged and laughing (emotion: joy, humor).

On further thought, you feel that this objective of inclusiveness is better achieved during the first part of the speech. It opens the door for the more profound emotions to be effective. These stronger emotions are what should constitute the final emotion.

You try to condense your understanding of the emotions you would like the audience to have at the end of the speech. Looking back at your notes, you realize that excitement and empowerment are the re-occurring emotions. You express the final emotions in a short paragraph: "An empowering feeling when you realize that you can make a difference in the lives of needy children and an exciting feeling that you have just seen a project that allows you to make that difference."

You suddenly grasp the magnitude of what that final emotion represents. If you feel this way, you are likely to be inspired and contribute to the cause. Now that you understand the emotions that need to be conveyed to your audience, you feel your job of writing a speech is a lot clearer. If you are able to communicate this feeling to your audience, they are likely to act in ways similar to you. This will help you meet the speech's objectives. You look back at the day's work and appreciate the clarity offered by understanding the final emotion. It was a good idea to spend the time developing it. You take a break and promise yourself to get back to writing the speech tomorrow.

The next day you go back and review Chapter 4 of *Emote* again. You turn your attention to the next important concept, the initial emotion. You learn in that chapter that understanding the initial emotion allows the speaker to meet the audience at their emotional state at the beginning of the speech. It also helps the speaker to understand the two ends of the emotional experience: the initial emotion and the final emotion. "Ah!" you think, "the concept of initial emotion makes sense."

The fundraiser will take place on Friday evening. The audience will be tired and looking for a relaxing outing with friends and members of their community. You envision a welcoming ambiance with light music and opportunity to socialize before the event begins. This is bound to help relax the audience.

Having been to many fundraisers yourself, you have always felt uncomfortable going to them when there is an expectation to "give." There are overt signs for donations and every second person you meet is reminding you that a generous donation would be very welcome. You do not want your audience to go through this experience. You believe that they will be more generous if they are free of any imposed expectations. You want them to give because they want to contribute, not because they are expected to do so. You think that some of this "mood setting" will have to be done before the speech begins.

You decide to work with the organizers to create an environment at the event that is aligned with how you want your audience to feel. You are not sure if they will understand or cooperate but you decide to give them a call to discuss the issue. To your surprise, the event chair is intrigued by your request and is very supportive. She suggests that the two of you meet to discuss details. This is a positive start.

Though the ambiance at the event will help relax the audience, you think about using the first half of your speech to put them at ease and establish a rapport. You want to take the pressure off, make them laugh, and forget their worries so that they can truly be there in the moment and absorb the emotions of your speech. If they do that, you plan to use the second half of the speech to evoke strong emotions that help them understand how their contributions will make a difference—that they can indeed make a difference. You hope they will step up and donate generously to the organization. You decide to take a break again and get back to preparations at the next opportunity.

The next day, you take stock of what has been accomplished so far. You understand how you would like your audience to feel at the end of the speech. You also have a clear idea of the mood you want to set at the beginning of the speech. Now you want to plan the emotional journey of the audience. You would like to explore two concepts that the author talks about in *Emote*. First, you would like to understand how the concepts of "hard" and "soft" emotions apply to your speech. Second, you would like to understand the emotional journey of the audience, not just the emotional end points of the speech. You decide to tackle the emotional journey first.

Chapter 4 in *Emote* discusses how emotional highs and lows in a speech help make it memorable as well as forces the audience to act. When strong emotional gradients—where emotions change from positive to negative or vice versa—are used well, they can significantly increase the impact of a speech. You think about how you can take the audience to a really low point, a frustrating feeling that comes when you are in a situation beyond your control, where you feel powerless in the face of insurmountable odds. You think this would be a strong negative emotion in the middle of the speech that will complement well the positive emotions at the end. In many ways, you want your audience to experience the emotions of the children they will be helping. These children are overwhelmed by their circumstances and do not see any light at the end of the tunnel. This hopelessness is what you would like the audience to feel. You make a mental note that the audience needs to be in the shoes of one of these children to feel like they do. This is going to be difficult to pull off, but you feel that the impact will be dramatic on your audience.

Next, you think about how much time to devote to each of these emotional experiences. In Chapter 3 of *Emote*, the author discusses a very interesting concept called soft and hard emotions. Emotions like love and joy are grouped as "soft" emotions because the impact on us is weaker and it takes time for the emotion to take hold. On the other hand, emotions like fear and grief are "hard" emotions because their impact on us is stronger, so much so that we can get emotionally drained if exposed to them for too long. These emotions have to be used with care. You find these distinctions fascinating and, to better understand this concept, you tabulate the emotions you have to work within your speech.

Part of Speech	Emotion	Kind of Emotion
The beginning.	Humor, calmness.	Positive, weak emotions.
During the middle.	Frustration, helplessness.	Strong, negative emotions.
Toward the end.	Excitement, empowerment.	Strong, positive emotions.

Based on this table, you decide that the first half of your speech would be entertaining and fun, working with the emotions of humor and endearment or other soft or neutral emotions. Toward the middle of the speech, you will start incorporating negative emotions and move your audience quickly toward the stronger negative emotions of frustration and helplessness. Beyond this emotional low point, the emotional journey will take a positive turn (typically, when the conflict is resolved) and you will take your audience toward the emotions of excitement and empowerment at the end of the speech. You will spend the last few minutes of your speech building on these positive emotions. This distribution of time to the various emotions will strike the right balance so that the audience will not be overwhelmed by the stronger emotions that are bound to come out as you put your audience in the shoes of these young, helpless kids. You also decide to introduce your own children in the first half of the story. Talking about your children is a sure way of connecting with the audience. They can relate and open up to take in the profound message that comes later. You also feel that it provides a good segue to the main character in your speech who is a child laborer.

You pause to summarize the emotional journey of your audience. Your thought is that, at the start of the evening, the audience will not be particularly excited. They will be tired after a week of work and apprehensive due to the expectations of donating at the fundraiser. You plan to start working on their emotional state even before the speech. You have worked with the event coordinator to set a welcoming and inclusive mood. All volunteers have been instructed not to purposefully bring up the topic of donations or expected donation amounts. The entire evening will be about meeting people, talking about family, and making people comfortable. Even the menu for the evening has been chosen such that it reminds people of a home-cooked meal. It will add to the feelings of being welcome and comfortable. You will build on this emotion in the first part of the speech and use stories that connect you to the audience, making them feel comfortable and ready to feel the strong emotions of your speech. You then engage them with your main story. The story describes the child's plight and then evokes strong emotions of helplessness and sympathy. Finally, you bring the audience back up emotionally as you resolve the conflict to end your story, leaving them with strong positive emotions of inspiration and empowerment. These emotions will make your message memorable and will catapult the audience to act.

You look back and realize the greatness of what you have achieved so far. You have planned the emotional journey of your audience during your speech. "This is remarkable," you think. "Now I just have to write a speech that delivers this emotional experience." But before you start that process, you decide to take a break.

You get back to your project the next day. It is now time to start writing the speech. You think about possible stories that you can use. You already have one in mind—it is the success story of Vijay, a former child laborer who was made to work 16 hours every day in inhumane conditions for almost no wages. Your organization got him out of those conditions, and he is free today and getting an education. This would make a good anchor story for the speech but there are aspects of writing a story that you are confused about. You decide to read Chapter 10 of *Emote*, "The Art of Telling a Story."

While reading the chapter, you make a few notes. You notice the three Cs of storytelling: character, conflict, and construction. You worry about your story not having a well-developed conflict. Could you write your story so that it introduces a conflict in your speech? You decide to spend some time exploring this idea. The author also emphasizes the importance of painting images using words because it enhances memory and helps with the flow of emotions. You think about the story and can identify parts where you can paint pictures with words.

To begin the speech, you think about adding some humor and then talking a little bit about your children. You feel that talking about them will endear you to the audience. They will be able to relate to your feelings of love and joy as you share your experience with your two children. It will also be a good transition to the main story of Vijay.

Finally, you think about the ending. The final emotions are clear to you, but what is the best way to deliver them? Clearly, the resolution of the conflict in your story will form an important bridge to bring the audience toward more positive emotions. You could further develop those emotions by conveying a profound message after the conflict is resolved. How will you convey this message for maximum impact? You take a few minutes to reflect back on Chapter 7, "The Words." The author talks about using rhyme as an excellent way to convey emotion. You like this idea because you have dabbled with poetry, and enjoy reading and composing poems. It's sad that your schedule has not allowed you to spend more time doing this, but this speech allows you to do just that. You decide to end the speech with a poem.

You take a step back and review the speech. You feel that it lacks a visual message that captures the meaning of your speech. You think about what that might be and come up with the image of a kite flying in the sky. You imagine how a kite with a broken string might represent kids without any support or help, flying aimlessly in life. On the other hand, a string tied to the kite can provide guidance and support so it can soar. You like this metaphor; it provides you with a visual representation of the soul of the speech and also helps you choose a story for the first part of it. You decide that you will share the story of flying a kite with your son in the first part of the speech.

You summarize how you will deliver the emotional journey you have planned for the audience. You will begin with a humorous anecdote about flying a kite with your son to build rapport. This will relax the audience and evoke the initial emotion. Then you will transition into Vijay's story. You will use this story to bring the audience to an emotional low. This lowest point will be related to the conflict introduced in the story. The resolution of this conflict will result in positive emotions being generated in the audience. You will develop these positive emotions and will finally leave the audience with the final emotion using a few lines of poetry.

Over the next few weeks, you spend a couple of hours a day developing the speech. You refer to *Emote* on many occasions to seek clarity. Finally, when the speech is ready, you feel it adequately captures the emotions you have tried to convey. Overall, you feel satisfied, but more importantly, transformed about how you write and deliver a speech. The promise of *Emote*, of providing a paradigm shift in verbal communication, has been kept.

|||||||||||||||||||||||||||||||||||||||||||||||||||||||||||||||||||||||||||||||||||||||||||||||||||||||

Kite in the Wind

Ladies and Gentlemen, honored guests, friends and colleagues, welcome to the annual dinner gala of Adarsh. I hope this evening will be a reminder to all of you of the responsibility we have and the opportunities that exist to make a difference. I hope it will be an evening to remember.

A few weeks ago, I got a fabulous gift from my three-year-old son. I was planning to spend a typical Sunday, sleep in a little bit, read the news, relax and cook some breakfast—except that this was not a typical Sunday. It was Father's Day. My three- and one-year-old kids, with some help from my wife, had stayed up late the night before to prepare a couple of cards. The cards were simple, a few drawings with "Happy Father's Day" written on them, but they were special cards for me—they were my first Father's Day cards. As I looked into their gleaming and mischievous eyes, I realized that they had just made a difference in my life. It didn't take money or a lot of effort, it just look love.

For all the adorable things they do, children also have a way of knowing when they have you in the palm of their hands. The very next thing my three-year-old said was, "Daddy, can we have some candy...pleeeease?" Children are the most wonderful thing that happen to you, yet they can also be the most frustrating. After two kids, I now have a new found respect for my parents. If I was even 50 percent like the brats I have, my parents have enormous reserves of patience.

These days, my three-year-old is fascinated by kites. We spend time making them and when they are ready, I hold one for him and then let it go just as he begins to run as fast as he can. The kite, behind him, soars high into the sky, majestic and balanced, my son's small hands giving it the stability and strength to fight the wind and fly. It is a magnificent sight.

Ladies and gentlemen, and esteemed guests, I hope you have had the pleasure of watching a kite fly high up in the sky. I often see my child in that kite soaring in the sky. If I can provide some stability and strength, I can see my son soar high in whatever he undertakes. But not all children in this world get the guidance and balance they need to succeed. Consider the story of Vijay, a young boy in a major city in India. He lives in a small house in a slum. His entire house is 200 square feet, half the size of your two-car garage. The roof is made of asbestos sheathing discarded by a factory. There are no windows, just enough space for a bed, a desk, a stove, and a makeshift toilet. There is no open space between his house and the neighbors on three sides. The entrance to the house is from a five-foot-wide street, which is strewn with litter and garbage. On the side of the street runs an open sewer, the stench of which would surely overwhelm a visitor. The houses are so close to each other that Vijay's home seems perpetually dark; no sunlight ever gets into it. His parents are old, and his siblings were married off. When his father lost his job a few years ago, they had no savings and there was no means of income. Finding no other alternative, Vijay started working in a garment factory at the tender age of 10. Vijay had been a good student and loved school—all that had to go because his family needed money.

The job at the garment factory was not easy. His day started at 9 a.m. and ended at 11 p.m. For 14 hours of work every day, he was given meals and a dollar. Most weeks he worked all seven days. Sometimes he would get a half day off on Sunday. Vijay was a smart boy and knew that he was not being treated fairly, but he was afraid. He was afraid that, if he quit this job, he may not get another one and then would have no way of feeding his elderly parents. And thus, he worked and worked and worked.

The garment factory was cramped, with hundreds of workers working close together. The air was not fresh, it was hot and humid, and the lights were dim. At night, when he was done, his back would hurt because of his bad posture, his shirt would be drenched from perspiration, his eyes would be burning from staring at intricate designs for 14 hours, his hands would be tired after working on the garments, but his spirit was never broken. He always left work with a smile, his dollar tucked safely in his pocket, and excited about coming back the next day.

Vijay was saved one day when a human rights organization, with the help of local police, raided the garment factory. They gathered the children and took them to a youth hostel. They cared for their families and Vijay finally got his break. Today, you can see Vijay smile as he studies for his class. His clothes are ordinary, but they are clean. He still lives with his elderly parents, but goes to school every day and works three hours every evening where his earnings are the same as working 16 hours in the garment factory. Vijay's life has changed for the better because of the compassion and love of the NGO that rescued him.

Would it surprise you to know that the NGO that rescued Vijay was none other than Adarsh? It should not, because Vijay is just one of many that we have helped. At Adarsh, we are in the business of helping children fly high like kites. For an amount less than the cost of your dinner today, we provide the balance and support so that they can make their dreams come true. How would you like to be at the other end of the string, helping a child fly like a kite in his or her life? Adarsh can give you the opportunity to make such an impact, to change lives, to help children like Vijay get out of the mediocrity and helplessness that surround them so they can envision a bold and better future for themselves. We make it possible for people like you in one part of the world to influence and correct human rights violations in other, poorer parts of the world. Adarsh connects humanity, so that the helpless are no longer alone but get a voice and strength from you, even though you are half a world away from them. We are your link to do good, to provide a semblance of humanity in places where none exist. We, ladies and gentlemen, help you make a difference in life, to leave a legacy, to help someone else fly like a kite.

I thought I knew that Vijay was thankful for what we have done for him, but I did not really understand how thankful he was until I met him earlier this year. The meeting left me a changed man as I understood how much I have and...how little of that I give to others. It left me a better father as I understood the difference I can make in the life of my children and, finally, it left me wanting to do more...because there is no better feeling than knowing that you made a difference in someone's life.

I urge you to join in our efforts, to contribute in whatever form you can, not because we want your money, but because I want you to feel how I felt when I met Vijay, to feel the depth of his appreciation, to feel that you made a difference in someone else's life.

Let me leave you with this message today:

There is nothing as beautiful as a kite in the wind,

But too many kids today are like kites with a broken string.

They are floundering; they are gasping for air.

They need your help, your guidance, your care.

So that together we can repair their strings,

And they, too, can fly like kites with wings.

With you holding their strings tight,

They will have that balance just right.

After all, there is nothing as beautiful as a kite in the wind.

Epilogue

The Three Speeches

In 2007, I won the World Championship of Public Speaking. To win this event, I had to write and deliver three different speeches. This requirement is Toastmasters International's way to ensure that their winner is not just "lucky" and can repeat his or her speaking performance. Competitors use different speeches in the quarter-finals, semi-finals, and the finals. I wanted to share with you the three speeches that I used to win the World Championship, the thoughts that led me to write them, and the process of preparing an important speech. A speech, when first conceived, is rarely as beautiful as it ends up. Sometimes, the final emotion or the key idea is the only thing that remains from the original version; the stories, characters, and flow change. This is why I have emphasized a move away from tools and concentration on the emotional journey.

I consider the first version of a speech when the final emotion has been identified. You may end up with multiple iterations before you get to this stage, but I don't count that as the first version of the speech. The process of refining this first draft into the final version of the speech is really where great speakers distinguish themselves. It requires not only skill in both writing and delivering a speech, but also a strong understanding of interpreting feedback and high emotional intelligence. If a speaker has thought about his emotional journey, he has a model of what a good speech should be like. The feedback allows him to compare this model of what he is trying to do to what the audience is telling him about his speech. The whole process of refining a speech is to get an alignment between the emotional journey of the audience and the journey that was planned by the speaker. On many occasions, feedback and evaluations don't tell the whole story. The speaker has to understand why her audience is feeling a certain way and then figure out what in her speech is making them feel that way. This process, though time consuming and frustrating, is one of the most rewarding experiences of public speaking.

I went through this process many times while preparing for the World Championship. Although you may never enter a speech competition, the insights that I gained will help you develop a good speech, even if it's just a simple report to your colleagues at work.

The Journey to the World Championship

The year 2007 started out as just another year. I was in my third year at MIT and my research in the field of vortex-induced vibrations had begun to produce some interesting results. My wife was working for a company in Cambridge after finishing her studies at Brown University. Things were going well.

I had also decided I would compete in the World Championship of Public Speaking for the fourth consecutive year. The previous year, I had taken third place in one of the 10 semi-finals in the competition. Though I had not won in 2006, the overwhelming feeling I had after my semi-final loss was that, with the right speech, I could reach the World Championship. It was not a matter of speaking skill; it was a matter of writing an impactful speech. This was also the time that I had finally begun to understand and develop the emotional approach to speaking. I was confident that this would help me make the jump to the World Championship.

Despite my success in 2006, writing my first speech in 2007 was difficult. I struggled for many months as I tried to identify a clear final emotion and a good story to convey it. After many months of work, and only a few weeks before the start of the competition, the speech finally began to take shape. I have always believed that contracts and legal documents do not define a relationship, business or personal. I wanted to convey this thought using the most important contract we get into: marriage. In my speech, called "Perfect," I proposed that a successful marriage is between two people who decide to make it work. Although compatibility, environmental conditions, and ambition all play a part, a marriage lasts because two people have decided that there is no way out of the contract. It has little to do with whether a marriage was arranged or whether two people fell in love.

I had identified a clear final emotion. I wanted my audience to feel empowered to make the best of their situations in life and not feel like victims to things beyond their control. My approach was to change the perspective of a Western audience on arranged marriage and then broaden this shift in perspective to other areas of life.

I thought I had the right story for this speech: my own. I had had an arranged marriage and was intrigued by the ongoing discussion, especially in Western societies, of arranged marriages versus choosing your partner for life. I felt sure that, if I was able to tap into this ongoing emotional dialogue, I could create an impactful speech. Though this conflict made for a very good speech, I had to be careful. I did not want to give the impression that one approach to marriage was better than the other. Instead, I decided to tell my story, share my learning, and find a way of having my learning apply in a more general context.

In the final version of the speech, I used many of the tools I describe in this book to take my audience on an emotional journey. In the beginning, I started the speech with a controversial statement—"Everything in life is arranged!"—that got the attention of the audience. I had a lot of humor in the first half of the speech, which helped me build rapport. It also helped me establish a positive emotion so that the profound message at the end would be more effective. The body of the speech had a well-developed conflict, an internal strife that everyone in the audience could identify with. Finally, at the end of the speech, the resolution of the conflict was satisfying and provided a profound message. I ended the speech with a poem to enable the final emotion to flow and be felt in a profound way.

I will now share the final version of the speech with you. Immediately following this speech, I will also share an earlier version of it. Though there were many improvements, two stand out. First, the flow of the speech is much improved. This directly helps in the flow of emotions and was a key reason for its success. Second, the conflict is better developed. In fact, there is almost no conflict in the first version. The conflict provides a lot of character to the speech, helping evoke strong emotions and leading to a profound ending.

‖‖

Perfect

Let me ask you a question that may seem a little strange—how many of you chose your parents? ...how about your kids? (some of you wish you had)... or your health problems...no...they just happened...my point is that, whether we like it or not, "everything in life is arranged." Mr. Contest Master, fellow Toastmasters, today I'm going to tell you about a time when something in my life was arranged, how that changed my life, and how the lesson that I learned will change your life too.

It was 2001, Houston, Texas, and I, having noticed the number of girls showing interest in me, had bowed to tradition.... Yes, friends, I was going to have an arranged marriage. I immediately discovered an unexpected benefit...it's a fantastic conversation starter. Just walk into a party and casually mention that you are going to have an arranged marriage...and see how the room is transformed. For the next 30 minutes, you will become the center of all attention...people will be fighting to get a glimpse of you...to make sure you actually exist.

In spite of all the attention, I was very scared. Was this the right thing to do? Should I wait till I find the "right girl" or should I let my parents in India find one for me...? One day, with these thoughts swirling in my mind, I decided to give my mother a call. "Hey, Mom, how are you going about looking for a girl for me?" I asked. "Don't worry, Vikas. This is my job. I look at many things—like the photograph."

"Yeah, and you consider only the most beautiful ones, right?"

"No, no, Vikas.... A boy and a girl should look good together."

[Terror in my eyes, I look at my face in a mirror.] "You've got to change this rule, Mom"...

"Vikas, this is my job. You just relax."

After several such "confidence boosting" conversations, Mom and Dad found a girl and surprisingly...I liked her. Mom did break her rule, though... Anjali was charming and beautiful.... In fact, so beautiful that, for once, I was sure that an arranged marriage was the way to go....

Finally, the day of the wedding arrived...three days of dancing and singing...with hundreds of people, most of whom I did not know and will never see again...countless ceremonies...it was quite an event...and, by the time it was over, I had just one thought in mind: "I am never going to do this again." No wonder the divorce rate in India is so low.... People will put up with anything to avoid going through the wedding again.

After the wedding, Anjali and I flew back to Texas...but I was still confused. Anjali was beautiful, educated, and cultured.... She was perfect for me...or was she?...What if she was not the right one?... What if I would have found the "perfect girl" if I had just waited?....What if? Friends, a few weeks into my marriage...I had been poisoned...poisoned by the "what if" question... And this doubt and regret started to choke the very meaning out of my life...because, you see, instead of strengthening my new marriage, I was already regretting it...until one day I was watching TV and some crazy guy came on and said, "Everything in life is arranged"....and I jumped up and said, "You better believe it."

Now, wait a minute, ladies and gentlemen, don't tell me you don't argue with your TV. You know what the best part about it is?.... You always win, because if you are losing you can shut it off and walk away...then this crazy man carried on: "Everything in life is arranged...until you make it perfect."

"What do you mean?" I shouted. The man continued, "You don't choose the country you were born in or the color of your skin or the relatives you have to deal with every day...but you have the choice to make things perfect." That day, for the first time, I lost an argument with my TV...but I realized that, if I wanted to have a perfect life, I won't get it by asking, "What if?"...I had to take whatever I had...and make it right. Today, five years later, my wife and I have a beautiful marriage.... Today, our arranged marriage is... perfect.

Friends, I don't know what life has to offer next...

And it may be way out of line

But there is no reason to fret and whine

For though you didn't cause your sorry plight

You do have the power to make it right

After all, everything in life is arranged...until you make it perfect.

II

Perfect [One of the First Versions]

"It's going to be arranged," Christie said, half falling out of her chair.... And then there was a long pause. "You're going to have an arranged marriage," she confirmed. "Yeah," I said...and her expression said it all. Her eyes were dripping with sympathy, "Oh you poor, poor boy. I feel so sorry for you."

Mr. Contest Master, fellow Toastmasters, and anyone of you who had dreamt of having an arranged marriage but did not have the courage to do so...let me tell you some of the many benefits of an arranged marriage. It's a fantastic conversation starter. Yeah...just walk into a party and casually mention, "I'm going to have an arranged marriage," and see how the room is transformed.... For the next half hour, you will be the center of all attention.... You will feel like a white elephant...rarely seen in public...and people will not be able to resist the opportunity to touch you and share your misery....

I do have to admit; for a brief period before my marriage, all this skepticism did get to me. I began to think, "What if these people are right? Should I wait till I find the 'right girl' for me? Should I rely on my parents for such a big decision?"... With these thoughts swirling in my mind, I called up my mother:

"Hey, mom, how are you going about looking for a girl for me?"'

"You should not worry about it," she answered. "There are many things that I look for—like the photograph for example."

"Yeah, you only consider the very beautiful ones, right?"

"No, no, Vikas...not at all. A boy and a girl should look good together—as a pair. The girl should possess the same level of beauty as the boy"....

[Look at a mirror...terror in my eyes.]

"We've got to change this rule, mom"...

"Don't worry, Vikas. This is my job. You just relax." As you can imagine, conversations like this did not do me any good.

Believe it or not, over the next year, Mom and Dad actually found a girl and, surprisingly...I liked her. Mom did break her rule though, because Anjali was charming and beautiful...in fact, so beautiful that, for once, I was saying... "I think arranged marriage is a great idea".... And the day of the marriage arrived. Over three days of dancing and singing under beautifully decorated shamiyanas with hundreds and hundreds of people...who you don't know and will never see again...giving you blessings...and pundits dressed in saffron-colored dhotis and uttering shlokhas in Sanskrit, and people showering you with flowers and rice...and, by the time it's done, the only thought I had was, "I'm never ever going to do this again"... Folks, I think the Indian marriage is designed with only one thing in mind...to make sure that you fear it so much, that you are going to put up with anything...so that you don't go through it again.

Once the marriage was over—we were left alone...talk about an awkward moment.... Here is a girl that I've talked to many times but never really spent time with in person...and suddenly we were man and wife...and the first few months were a challenge. We worked hard to understand the other person and soon we had a flourishing marriage...two people who genuinely cared about each other...about their goals, and were excited about their future. Our arranged marriage was now...perfect.

Life teaches you in strange ways, and I really did not understand the main lesson from all of this until a few years ago. [Story goes here.]

A lot of the things in my life were arranged—I didn't choose the country I was born in, I didn't choose the color of my skin, and, most of the time, I don't choose the problems I face— what I do choose is to make them perfect.

Friends, a lot of us are living our lives complaining that it was arranged... that we did not get to choose the best partner, the best company, the best job, and the best country...failing to realize that you have the power in your hands...to make it perfect.

Your life is arranged...only until you choose to make it perfect.

||||||||||||||||||||||||||||||||||||||||||||||||||||||||||||||||||||||||||||||||||||||||||||||||||||||

The second speech, which I used in the semi-finals, was called "Postcard." I wrote it in 2006, a year before I won the World Championship. While writing this speech, many of the concepts I discuss in *Emote* started coming together. In many ways, the writing of "Postcard" was the genesis of the concepts discussed in this book.

The speech was prompted by a strong feeling I often have that I am not living my life to the fullest. I believe that I can do more, be more, and care more for others, if only I could operate at my best all the time. I would be surprised if you do not have similar feelings at least some of the time. I believe that this is because *I rarely live in the moment*. When I'm in the office, I constantly think about all the things I should be doing at home, like spending time with my wife, making sure that all the bills are going out on time, and doing household chores. On the other hand, when I was at home, I would constantly worry about my work and plan things that I would do the next day in the office.

I believe that many are like me, struggling to live in the moment. I wanted to write a speech that would make my audience members change their lives and start living in the moment, to realize that the world is *now* and it is beautiful, to live rather than to always plan to live. I wrote "Postcard" to make a difference.

The message of this speech can be explained in one sentence: *Life should be lived in the moment.* This is not a new message and you have probably heard it before. What makes it memorable is the way it was delivered in "Postcard." The final emotion is strong, developed using stories that show what can happen if life is not lived in the moment. It leaves the audience with an overwhelming, sinking feeling of "I do not want to live my life like this." "Postcard" is profound, and its impact has a stunning effect on the audience.

Like "Perfect," "Postcard" uses many of the tools discussed in this book. I begin my speech with a dialogue that immediately engages the audience. The speech has two stories: the first is a hilarious incident at the Taj Mahal, and the second is a personal story about the passing away of my uncle. Both stories are woven together using the postcard theme. I paint many images, none more important than that of the postcard that is tied to the theme of the speech. Lastly, the finale is dramatic, capturing the strongest emotions at the end of the speech.

"Postcard" calls for life-changing decisions. It asks its audience to look at how they live their lives, to understand and appreciate the present, and not to live in the future. The challenge is not just to convince the audience to live in the moment, but to accomplish the significantly more challenging task of leaving them with so much emotional energy at the end to enable those big changes. This is what makes "Postcard" an effective speech.

As with "Perfect," I share with you an earlier version of the speech ("Taj Mahal Story"). Though the earlier version captures the spirit of the speech, the flow, particularly toward the end, is not very good. This adversely impacts the ability to convey emotions in the speech. The use of the postcard as a central theme running through it has not been developed. You will notice that I try to end the speech with a poem, for reasons that I have discussed earlier. However, in practice with different groups, I received feedback that the strongest emotions occurred when my uncle passes away and the impact of those strong emotions reduced the longer I spoke after that point. The final version tries to leave the audience at an emotional high point by moving to the end quickly, almost abruptly, after the end of the story. It took me over a week of constant work to write this unusual ending, which maximized impact. It is an unusual way to end a speech but proved to be very effective.

||||||||||||||||||||||||||||||||||||||||||||||||||||||||||||||||||||||||||||||||||||||||||||||||

Postcard

"Have you seen the Taj Mahal?" Jamie asked. I was used to this question. As soon as someone found out I was from India, this was the second question they asked me—the first one always being, "Did you have an arranged marriage?"

And so, I had a prepared answer. "It's beautiful," I replied.

The truth was that I had not seen the Taj Mahal but I was too embarrassed to admit it...so I learned to describe it from a postcard.

Mr. Contest Master, fellow Toastmasters, and anyone who claims to have seen a monument based on a postcard—it works. I had a great discussion with Jamie about the Taj Mahal, but this was the straw that broke the camel's back.

Two years ago when my wife and I visited India, we planned a trip to the Taj Mahal. Both of us were so excited; we told everyone about it—all our relatives and friends knew we were going to the Taj Mahal. When my favorite Uncle Jay found out we were going there, he had just one piece of advice, "Be careful of pickpockets. They are like magicians. They could get your wallet out even when you had your hand on it."

And not just him, all my aunts and cousins said the same thing...so when I was at the Taj Mahal, that's all I could think about. In fact, every 30 seconds my hand would automatically drift to my back pocket just to make sure that my wallet was there. That afternoon, while standing in line to buy a drink, I got engrossed in a discussion with my wife and our guide and, just for a few minutes, my mind wandered. And when my hand went back, my wallet was gone.

How could this be? I had been so careful. I turned around and shouted, "Someone stole my wallet!"

In just an instant, the hundred or so people around us were galvanized, their eyes darting from one corner to another for anything suspicious. The thief could not be far. As I was desperately looking around, I heard the voice of my driver, "Sirji, Sirji!"

"What?" I shouted.

"It's in your hand."

And sure enough, it was in my hand. I immediately realized what had happened. I had taken it out to buy the drink and, when my other hand touched my pocket, I immediately assumed that someone stole it...because that's what I had been thinking about the whole time.

I can never forget this incident because of two reasons. One, my wife won't let me forget it. It has too much entertainment value for her. And two, because of how I felt that evening.

I had just spent the day in front of one of the most beautiful structures built by man, but I couldn't recall the touch of the radiant white marble or the elaborate carvings on the pillars. I didn't remember the smell of the flowers that surrounded the structure or the details of the spectacular dome. It was almost like I had just seen a...postcard.

My day felt incomplete, like I had missed something. But it took a phone call to make me realize what. It was the 15th of March. It was early in the morning and the phone rang—my mother was on the line. "I have bad news, Vikas. Uncle Jay passed away."

I was shocked...my favorite uncle...gone.

"But Mom, the doctor gave him six months. How could he be gone?"

"Well, doctors can be wrong, you know...."

"He can't be gone, Mom."

"He's dead, Vikas...."

"But Mom, I was almost done with my project. I finally had some time to call him."

Tears rolled down my cheeks as I remembered the wonderful years I had spent with him when I was a kid. I saw myself playing in his small house in Calcutta, those hot summer days I spent playing in his backyard, his caring hug, his gentle smile. As these images raced across my mind, I realized for the first time that I had lived my whole life like a...postcard. Flat and incomplete. I had always been so busy building the future that I had never lived in the moment. The moment that had the smell, the touch, the sound, and the emotion. The moment that is gone in a snap. Forever, just like Uncle Jay was gone...forever.

Friends, there are too many of us who live our lives worrying about our wallet and forget to enjoy the magnificence of the Taj Mahal in front of us. Not realizing that if we fail to capture the moment—the sound, the smell, the touch, and the feeling—what remains is a picture without a soul, a memory without emotion...just a postcard.

Your life is much more than a simple...postcard.

|||||||||||||||||||||||||||||||||||||||||||||||||||||||||||||||||||||||||||||||||||||||||||||||||||||||||

How do you feel? Do you have that sinking feeling that I had talked about earlier? You will be surprised how many times people come up to me and say that this speech changed their lives or that this is the best speech that they have heard. It is not that these people have not heard about living in the moment before. This is an old topic for an inspirational speech. However, they probably have never felt the emotions that this speech brings forth.

I want to discuss further why this speech is so effective. Notice that it does not give you a solution. It does not tell you that this is how you live in the moment or that this is what you should do every day to get the most out of your life. The speech just makes you realize that everything is not right. You are not living in the moment and you need to change that. Because it leaves you at an emotional high, you have a lot of energy and hence you will make a change in your life to "make it right."

I often get the comment after people hear this speech that something is not right with the ending, as if it was not supposed to end there. In some sense, they are saying that the ending is too abrupt. When I ask them if they felt that the message is not clear, they agree that the message is clear: it's just a feeling that they have. The ending was left abrupt for a reason. The speech is what I call a "life changer." It is designed to motivate listeners to make some changes so to get the most out of their lives.

If I write a speech that asks you to change your life and leaves you with a very contented feeling, you will not do anything about it. You might say "nice speech" and then go on with your old ways. The reason this speech is so effective is because it makes you feel uncomfortable. It leaves you with a feeling that everything is not okay in your life and that is why you will do something about it. This speech targets emotion aimed to produce powerful results.

||||||||||||||||||||||||||||||||||||||||||||||||||||||||||||||||||||||||||||||||||||||||||||||||||||||

Taj Mahal Story

"Have you seen the Taj Mahal?" Jamie asked. I was used to this question. As soon as someone found out I was from India, this was the second question they asked me—the first one always being, "Did you have an arranged marriage?" And so, I was prepared. "Isn't it beautiful?" I replied. The truth was that I had not seen the Taj Mahal but I was too embarrassed to admit it. How could I tell someone that I spent 22 years of my life in India and did not see the Taj Mahal when people come from all over the world to see it...so I learned to describe it from pictures.

Mr. Contest Master, fellow Toastmasters, and anyone who claims to have seen a monument based on a photograph—it works. This time, too, I got away with it, but this was the straw that broke the camel's back. I decided that, the next time I go to India, I will see the Taj Mahal...and so, a couple of years ago when my wife and I were in India, we planned a visit to the Taj Mahal.

We were so excited; we told everyone about it—all our relatives and friends knew we were going to the Taj Mahal...and they just had one thing to say—be careful of pickpockets. "These pickpockets were very skillful," they told us, "almost magicians. They could get your wallet out even when you had your hand it." And on and on they went.... So when I was at the Taj Mahal, that's all I could think about. In fact, every 30 seconds my hand would automatically drift to the back of my pocket just to make sure that my wallet was there. While standing in line to buy a drink, I got into a discussion with my wife and our guide and, just for a few minutes my mind was diverted, and when my hand automatically reached back...my wallet was gone. How could this be? I couldn't let the thief get away with it...not after I had been so careful. I whisked around and shouted, "Someone stole my wallet!" In an instant, the hundred or so people around us were galvanized...their eyes darting from one corner to another for anything suspicious... The thief could not be far.

As I was desperately looking around, I heard the voice of my driver, "Sirji, Sirji!"

"What?" I shouted.

"It's in your hand"...and sure enough, it was in my hand. I immediately realized what had happened. I had taken it out to buy the drink and, when my other hand unconsciously touched my pocket and found the wallet missing, I immediately assumed that someone stole it...because that's what I had been thinking about the whole time. At that moment, I looked at the hundreds of people who were around me...and they were all staring at me trying to figure out what I had been drinking.

I managed to hang on to my wallet for the rest of the day, but at the end I remember feeling a little strange. You know, I had just spent the day at the Taj Mahal and I didn't remember what it smelled like; I couldn't recall how it felt to touch the white marble. It was almost like I had only seen a picture.

I can never forget this incident because of two reasons: one, my wife won't let me forget it...it has too much entertainment value for her...and second, because of what happened on the 15th of March last year.

It was early in the morning and the phone rang. I was up already. My mother was on the line. "I have bad news, Vikas. Uncle Jay passed away."

I was shocked. "But Mom, the doctor gave him six months. How could he be gone...."

"Well, doctors can be wrong you know...."

"He can't be gone, mom."

"He's dead, Vikas...."

"But Mom...I was almost done with my project; I finally had some time to call him."

Tears rolled down my eyes as I remembered the wonderful years I had spent with him when I was a kid. I saw myself playing in his small house in Calcutta; my thoughts went back to those hot summer days we spent with him. As these images raced across my mind, I realized for the first time that my whole life had been like my visit to the Taj Mahal. I was so busy trying to create a nonexistent future that I failed to see the miracles right in front of me, the smell of the roses, and the love of our family and friends.

Let me leave you with this thought today:

There are times when we get in the rat race

And forget to enjoy every day we face

So we live in the future or in the past

But the present is where the die is cast

So from today live your life in this simple way

Just remember to enjoy your Taj Mahal every day.

||||||||||||||||||||||||||||||||||||||||||||||||||||||||||||||||||||||||||||||||||||||||||||||||||||

My success at the semi-final in 2007 meant I now had the privilege to compete in the finals of the World Championship of Public Speaking. I would be one of 10 finalists, each of whom, having gone through months of preparation, would have the opportunity to win one of the most coveted trophies in the world of public speaking. I knew the next few weeks would be intense and exciting. I also knew that I had very little time to write one of the best speeches of my life.

During the first few days of my preparation, I remember sitting down every day for hours in my bedroom in Cambridge, Massachusetts and just thinking about a purpose, a strong message that I could convey to my audience. After considerable thought and introspection, I decided that the emotion I most wanted to leave my audience with was conveyed best by the question, "Who are you?" Many years ago, when I had asked myself this question, I was filled with emotions of utter confusion and extreme disappointment. I had realized that I did not know who I was; I did not know my passions, my strengths, my dreams, and most important of all, I did not know my potential. Looking back, I now realize I also did not have the courage and confidence that automatically comes when you have started to answer this question. I decided that this question was going to be my gift to the world, the question that had helped me find my potential. My hope was that it would do the same for many others.

I am sure the fact that I was at MIT influenced the message I was trying to deliver. My journey to this hallowed institution had been a study in finding my potential. I could not think of a better story to use than my own to convey the message of my speech.

Throughout the preparation phase, I was dogged by the comparison of "The Swami's Question" to "Postcard." Time and time again, in feedback after a practice session, I was told that this speech was not as good as "Postcard." That phase made me realize the importance of writing a good speech once, because it becomes the gold standard for those that follow. Your audience will demand the same level of excellence forever afterward. It was an important lesson for me and one that can help all of us.

"The Swami's Question" takes the audience on a journey with me as I discover my potential in academics. They feel my trials and tribulations, triumphs and jubilations, as I work my way from a good student to an excellent one. The story, of course, culminates in my acceptance to graduate school at MIT. But the speech does not end there. That was not the final emotion I wanted to convey. At this juncture, I turn the spotlight on the audience and I ask them the very same deep questions that I had asked myself when my journey began, knowing well that they will not have the answers. But those feelings of utter confusion and disappointment were the emotions I wanted to convey.

As before, I am including an earlier version of the speech ("The Contest"). The title, "The Swami's Question," was suggested by a dear friend very late in the preparation phase. As I have mentioned on many occasions, you will see that only the soul, or final emotion, remained between the first and final versions. Many of the tools were changed to improve the flow and increase the emotional impact.

||||||||||||||||||||||||||||||||||||||||||||||||||||||||||||||||||||||||||||||||||||||||||||

The Swami's Question

My hands were shaking, my throat was dry... [holding an envelope]. In my hands was a letter that was going to change my life... Would it be for better...or worse... The answer was inside.

I stared at the return address: Massachusetts Institute of Technology— the graduate school of my dreams. Would it begin with "Congratulations" or "You've got to be kidding"?... The answer was inside.

My mind drifted back to when it all began...14 years ago.

Mr. Contest Master, fellow Toastmasters, and anyone here who remembers being a teenager, the year was 1989.... I was a teenager and my parents were desperate...sounds familiar, doesn't it! College was just a few years away and my grades...not there. My parents had been brilliant students...and clearly very trusting of each other, because they ruled out any problems with my genes...but having tried everything...from tutoring to mentoring...pleading to threatening ...they turned to the supernatural...the Swami.

One afternoon, Mom and I traveled to the old part of the city of Calcutta, India.... Here, the houses were so close that sunlight was a myth.... The aroma of spices drifted in the hot, humid air and here, in a small hut, sat the holy man everyone called the Swami.... His saffron robe drenched in sweat...he tried solve the problems people put before him. "Swami, Vikas has lot of potential...but the grades are not good," my mother pleaded...to which the Swami replied, "Meditation...try meditation"...and in a flash, his attention was on the next person.

I really did not believe in this meditation stuff, but one look at my mom... [look at her and show a frightened look] and I knew I would have to give it a try...but then I got hooked. Did you know that meditation is cool? Yeah... when my friends found out that I was into meditation...my popularity shot up like Apple's stock.... I was really enjoying all the attention...but behind closed doors, my meditation practice was in trouble.... Sitting in a quiet room with my eyes closed should be easy...except I could not stay awake. Within a few moments of closing my eyes, I was sleeping like a baby.... But meditation had made me so popular that I had to find a way around it.... So Mom and I went back to the Swami.... "Ask yourself a question...who are you?"

Have you ever looked at modern art and wondered...so, which side is up?.... My visit to the Swami was equally confusing.... Over the next few months, I tried to answer the Swami's question...and, miraculously, my grades improved so much that I was accepted into a good undergraduate program in India.

Freshman year of college—what's not to love about it? Meditation was out and in came...girls!!!... Then came my first semester grades.... It felt like life had kicked me in the stomach...so hard that I was left gasping for air and begging for answers, and in the months that followed, my desperate attempts to bounce back only made me question my own abilities until one day, tired, frustrated, I closed my eyes and returned to the Swami's question.... "Who are you?"...and, in that deep silence, I heard the music of my dreams, the song of my talents, the symphony of my spirit...and I finally understood what the Swami had done.... Meditation was just a tool to make me stop and listen, because the answer was not out there.... The answer was inside.

Fourteen years later, once again the answer had been inside [pointing to the envelope]. It did begin with congratulations!... I had fulfilled my dream... all because the Swami showed me that the answer is not in that magic pill or with Dr. Phil.... The answer is always...inside.

Friends, have you ever looked inside?... What if the answer to your problems is not outside?... What if your answer [action only for inside].

What the Swami asked me then, I ask you now..."Who are you?"

IIIIIIIIIIIIIIIIIIIIIIIIIIIIIIIIIIIIIIIIIIIIIIIIIIIIIIIIIIIIIIIIIIIIIIIIIIIIIIIIIIIIIIIIIIIIIIII

IIIIIIIIIIIIIIIIIIIIIIIIIIIIIIIIIIIIIIIIIIIIIIIIIIIIIIIIIIIIIIIIIIIIIIIIIIIIIIIIIIIIIIIIIIIIIIII

The Contest

Who am I? Have you ever pondered over this question?... In Eastern mythology, saints meditated for years to be able to answer this question...

Mr. Contest Master, fellow Toastmasters, and especially everyone who has ever asked themselves this question...get some work...at least that's what I would have said 10 years ago.

The first semester, I gave it everything I had. I worked long hours...I slept little and talked even less...and when the final results came in, I was second... from the bottom. "Devastated" was too mild a word to describe my emotional state at that time...but I had read enough self-help books to realize that this was necessary...to help make a stronger, more complete me. I got up...wiped my tears...and jumped back to work.... I cut down the little social life that I had...removed the few hours of sports I played every week.... Ladies and gentlemen, I paid the price...and when the results came in that semester...I was still second...from the bottom.

By this time, I was looking for answers...I was grabbing at straws...and one day a friend suggested that I meditate. "Sure," I said....

The first few days, I closed my eyes and...went to sleep. I couldn't help but ask, "How this was helpful?"

"Hey, man, the only thing that happens is that I sleep well...and a lot,"
I told my friend. "Keep trying," he said...so I kept trying and, one day, I did
not sleep.

I started having conversations with myself. It's interesting that we spend
years trying to build relationships with our friends, decades trying to figure
out our spouses, a lifetime understanding our kids, but not even a few mo-
ments building a relationship with ourselves.

Strangely, my grades started to go up...and I was actually working less.

I was always competing...until I realized that my only competitor was
"me."

Know yourself.

Friends, most of us will never live to our potential, not because we did
not try hard enough or that we cannot, but because we never spent the time
to know ourselves and hence know our potential.

||||||||||||||||||||||||||||||||||||||||||||||||||||||||||||||||||||||||||||||||||||||||||||||||||||

Conclusions

I sometimes learn better when I see concrete applications of the concepts being discussed. If you are the same, I hope this chapter has been beneficial for you. The three speeches I used to with the World Championship
in 2007 used many of the ideas I have discussed in this book. I hope you
will review them when you feel the need for concrete examples of a concept
I discuss in *Emote*.

It is a great feeling when people remember a speech many years after
you have delivered it. All three of these speeches fall into that category.
To this day, I get e-mails from Toastmasters' members who watch "The
Swami's Question" on DVD and consider it a model speech. I still meet
people who heard me deliver "Postcard" many years ago and tell me that
they no longer live their lives like a postcard. I hope you get to feel the way
I do when I hear these comments. This book can make that happen.

Bibliography

Achatz, Grant, and Nick Kokonas. *Life, on the Line: A Chef's Story of Chasing Greatness, Facing Death, and Redefining the Way We Eat.* New York: Gotham, 2011.

Allen, Collin. "Mirror, Mirror in the Brain, What's the Monkey Stand to Gain?" *NOU^ S* 44:2 (2010) 372–391.

Aristotle. *The Art of Rhetoric.* Translated by Hugh Lawson-Tancred. London: Penguin, 1991.

———. *Rhetoric.* A hypertextual resource compiled by Lee Honeycutt. *http://rhetoric.eserver.org/aristotle/.*

———. *Rhetoric.* Translated by W. Rhys Roberts. *http://classics.mit.edu//Aristotle/rhetoric.html.*

"ASME 2010 29th International Conference on Ocean, Offshore and Arctic Engineering 29th International Conference on Ocean, Offshore and Arctic Engineering: Volume 6." White paper. Shanghai, China, June 6–11, 2010.

Atwater, Eastwood. *I Hear You: A Listening Skills Handbook.* New York: Walker, 1992.

Ben-Ze'ev, Aharon. *The Subtlety of Emotions*. Cambridge, Mass.: MIT, 2000: 39.

Blaine, Gerald, and Lisa McCubbin. *The Kennedy Detail: JFK's Secret Service Agents Break Their Silence*. New York: Gallery, 2010.

Boyd, Anderson. Quoted in "Satyajit Ray (1921–1992)" by Vijay Mishra. *www.mcc.murdoch.edu.au/ReadingRoom/5.2/Mishra.html*.

Bradberry, Travis, and Jean Greaves. *Emotional Intelligence 2.0*. San Diego, Calif.: TalentSmart, 2009.

Brown, Roger, and James Kulik. "Flashbulb memories," *Cognition*, Volume 5, Issue 1, 1977, pages 73-99. *www.sciencedirect.com/science/article/pii/001002777790018X*.

Bryant, Gregory A., and H. Clark Barrett. "Vocal Emotion Recognition Across Disparate Cultures." *Journal of Cognition and Culture* 8.1 (2008): 135–48.

Cain, Susan. *Quiet: The Power of Introverts in a World That Can't Stop Talking*. New York: Crown, 2012.

Carnegie, Dale, and Dorothy Carnegie. *The Quick and Easy Way to Effective Speaking*. New York: Association, 1962.

Charan, Ram. "The Discipline of Listening." Blog post: *http://blogs.hbr.org/cs/2012/06/the_discipline_of_listening.html*.

Cherniss, Cary, and Daniel Goleman. *The Emotionally Intelligent Workplace: How to Select for Measure, and Improve Emotional Intelligence in Individuals, Groups, and Organizations*. San Francisco, Calif.: Jossey-Bass, 2001.

Churchill, Sir Winston. "The Scaffolding of Rhetoric." *www.winstonchurchill.org/images/pdfs/for_educators/THE_SCAFFOLDING_OF_RHETORIC.pdf*.

Collins, Nick. "Smells can trigger emotional memories, study finds." (January 28, 2012) *www.telegraph.co.uk/science/science-news/9042019/Smells-can-trigger-emotional-memories-study-finds.html*.

Covey, Stephen R. *The 7 Habits of Highly Effective People*. New York: Free Press, 2004.

Crouching Tiger, Hidden Dragon. Director, Ang Lee. Sony Picture Classics, 2000.

De Fornari, Oreste. *Sergio Leone: The Great Italian Dream of Legendary America*. Rome: Gremese International, 1997.

Dolan, Gabrielle, and Yamini Naidu. Introduction. *Hooked: How Leaders Connect, Engage and Inspire with Storytelling*. Richmond, Va.: Wiley, 2013.

Doumont, Jean-luc. *Trees, Maps, and Theorems: Effective Communication for Rational Minds*. Kraainem, Belgium: Principiæ, 2009.

Duarte, Nancy. *Resonate: Present Visual Stories That Transform Audiences*. Hoboken, N.J.: Wiley, 2010.

———. *Slide:ology: The Art and Science of Creating Great Presentations*. Beijing: O'Reilly Media, 2008.

Dunn, Susan. "How an Introvert Can Survive Giving a Presentation." Career-Intelligence.com. *www.career-intelligence.com/management/ How-an-Introvert-Can-Survive-Giving-a-Presentation.asp*.

Ekman, Paul. *Emotions Revealed: Recognizing Faces and Feelings to Improve Communication and Emotional Life*. New York: Times, 2003.

Ernst, Bruno. *The Magic Mirror of M.C. Escher*. Taschen, 2007.

Escher, M.C. *Metamorphose*. Painting. May, 1937.

Eysenck, Hans J. *The Biological Basis of Personality*. Springfield, Ill.: Thomas, 1967.

Fisher, Roger, and Daniel Shapiro. *Beyond Reason: Using Emotions as You Negotiate*. New York: Viking, 2005.

Fiske, Susan. "Where Fear Lives." *Psychology Today*. September, 2002, page 74.

Fox, Elaine. *Emotion Science: Cognitive and Neuroscientific Approaches to Understanding Human Emotions*. Basingstoke: Palgrave Macmillan, 2008.

Fredberg, Tobias, and Flemming Norrgren. "What Do Good Global Leaders Do?" *Harvard Business Review* Blog. January 19, 2012.

Frey, James N. *How to Write a Damn Good Novel: A Step-by-Step No Nonsense Guide to Dramatic Storytelling*. New York: St. Martin's, 1987.

Frijda, Nico H. *The Emotions*. Cambridge, Mass.: Cambridge UP, 1986.

Gallo, Carmine. "Why Leadership Means Listening." *Businessweek Online* (2007): 30. Business Source Complete. Web. July 23, 2013.

Gladis, Stephen D. "Notes Are Not Enough." *Training and Development Journal*. Aug (1985): 35–38.

Glover, Dennis. *The Art of Great Speeches: And Why We Remember Them.* Cambridge: Cambridge University Press, 2011.

Godin, Seth. *Really Bad Power Point (and How to Avoid It).* Web: *www.sethgodin.com/freeprize/reallybad-1.pdf.*

Goleman, Daniel, Richard E. Boyatzis, and Annie McKee. "Primal Leadership: Realizing The Power of Emotional Intelligence." / Daniel Goleman, Richard Boyatzis, Annie Mckee. n.p.: Boston, Mass.: Harvard Business School Press, c2002., 2002. Classic Catalog. Web. 23 July, 2013.

Goleman, Daniel. "What Makes a Leader?" *Harvard Business Review* 76.6 (1998): 93–102. Scopus. Web. 23 July, 2013.

———. *Emotional Intelligence.* New York: Bantam, 1995.

The Great Debaters. Director, Denzel Washington. MGM, 2000.

Gross, James J., and Robert W. Levenson. "Emotion Elicitation Using Films." *Cognition & Emotion* 9.1 (1995): 87–108.

Gross, Terry. *Fresh Air.* "Grant Achatz: The Chef Who Lost His Sense Of Taste." (July 14, 2011.) *www.npr.org/player/v2/mediaPlayer.html?action =1&t=1&islist=false&id=134195812&m=134195976.*

Harris Interactive Survey. "The Top Business Schools: Recruiters' M.B.A. Picks." *Wall Street Journal*, September 20, 2006. Web: *http://online.wsj.com/page/2_1245.html.*

Hartelius, E. Johanna. *The Rhetoric of Expertise.* Lanham: Lexington, 2010. 34.

Heath, Chip, and Dan Heath. *Made to Stick: Why Some Ideas Survive and Others Die.* New York: Random House, 2007.

Hertz, Dr. Rachel. Interviews with Ira Flatow on *Talk of the Nation.* Web: *http://rachelherz.com/Blog_Interviews_News.html.*

Howard, Gregory T. *Dictionary of Rhetorical Terms.* Thorofare, N.J.: Xlibris, 2010. 171–172.

Hughes, Dennis. "Daniel Goleman on Emotions and Your Health." Shareguide.com. *www.shareguide.com/Goleman.html.*

An Inconvenient Truth. Director, Davis Guggenheim. Producers, Laurie David, Lawrence Bender, and Scott Z. Burns. Paramount Pictures Corp., 2006.

Isaacson, Walter. "The iPhone." *Steve Jobs*. New York: Simon & Schuster, 2011. 100–20.

Johnson, Debra L., John S. Wiebe, Sherri M. Gold, Nancy C. Andreasen, Richard D. Hichwa, G. Leonard Watkins, and Laura L. Boles Ponto. "Cerebral Blood Flow and Personality: A Positron Emission Tomography Study." *American Journal of Psychiatry* 156.2 (1999): 252–57.

Jourard, Sidney, and J.E. Rubin. "Self-disclosure and touching: A study of two modes of interpersonal encounter and their interrelation" (1968). *Journal of Humanistic Psychology*, 8, 39–48.

Kagan, Jerome. *What Is Emotion?: History, Measures, and Meanings*. New Haven, Conn.: Yale UP, 2007.

Keller, Helen. *The Story of My Life*. Dover Thrift Editions, 1996.

Kennedy, George A. "A Hoot in the Dark: The Evolution of General Rhetoric." *Philosophy & Rhetoric*. Vol. 25, No. 1 (1992), pp. 1–21.

Kennedy, John F. Inauguration address. *www.youtube.com/watch?v=BLmiOEk59n8*. Full text available at *http://www.bartleby.com/124/pres56.html*.

Kensinger, Elizabeth A. *Emotional Memory Across the Adult Lifespan*. New York: Psychology, 2009.

King, C. L. "Beyond Persuasion: The Rhetoric of Negotiation in Business Communication." *Journal of Business Communication* 47.1 (2009): 69–78.

LaCroix, Darren. "Ouch." Speech given in the 2001 World Championship of public speaking. Auburn, Mass. August 25, 2001.

Lamon, Dana. Personal communication with the author.

LaNae', Asha, and Trisha LaNae'. "A Conversation with Dr. Maya Angelou." *http://mayaangelou.com/news/13/*.

Leighton, Stephen R. "Aristotle and the Emotions." *Phronesis*. Vol. 27, No. 2 (1982), pp. 144–171.

Leinberger, Charles. *Ennio Morricone's The Good, the Bad and the Ugly: A Film Score Guide*. Lanham, Md.: Scarecrow, 2004.

Lidwell, William, Kritina Holden, and Jill Butler. *Universal Principles of Design*. Gloucester, Mass.: Rockport, 2003.

Longfellow, Henry Wadsworth. *Hyperion; And, Kavanagh*. Boston: Houghton, Mifflin, 1886. page 135.

Luperfoy, Susann (then Director of the UPOP program). Personal correspondence with the author.

The Mahabharata. Translated by Kisari Mohan Ganguli. *www.sacred-texts.com/hin/m12/m12c020.htm*.

Manzoor, Sarfraz. "Malcolm Gladwell: 'Speaking Is Not an Act of Extroversion.'" *The Guardian*. *www.theguardian.com/books/video/2010/jun/21/malcolm-gladwell*.

Maxwell, John C. *Leadership Gold: Lessons Learned from a Lifetime of Leading*. Nashville, Tenn.: Thomas Nelson, 2008.

McBride, Terry. Talk on music copyright. *www.youtube.com/watch?v=SQOWNU5-nNs*.

Medina, John. *Brain Rules: 12 Principles for Surviving and Thriving at Work, Home, and School*. Seattle, Wash.: Pear, 2008.

Morris, Larry Wayne. *Extraversion and Introversion: An Interactional Perspective*. New York: John Wiley and Sons, 1980.

Morrison, Terri, and Wayne A. Conaway. *Kiss, Bow, or Shake Hands: The Bestselling Guide to Doing Business in More than 60 Countries*. Avon, Mass.: Adams Media, 2006.

Murad, Mohammed. Personal communication with the author.

Navarro, Joe, and Marvin Karlins. *What Every BODY Is Saying: An Ex-FBI Agent's Guide to Speed-reading People*. New York: Collins Living, 2008.

Nichols, Ralph G., and Leonard A. Stevens. "Listening to People." *Harvard Business Review* (September, 1957): 85-92.

Nichols, Ralph G. "Listening Is Good Business." *Management of Personnel Quarterly* 1.2 (1962): 2–10. Business Source Complete. Web. July 23, 2013.

Oatley, Keith, and Jennifer M. Jenkins. *Understanding Emotions*. Cambridge, Mass.: Blackwell, 1996.

Palencik, J. T. "William James and the Psychology of Emotion: From 1984 to the Present." *Transactions of the Charles S. Peirce Society*, Vol. 43, No. 4 (2007).

Pausch, Randy, and Jeffrey Zaslow. *The Last Lecture*. New York: Hyperion, 2008.

Peter, Jennifer. "Remembering the Challenger disaster." *www.youtube. com/watch?v=_ZIDRKcxso8*.

Plutchik, Robert, and Henry Kellerman. *Emotion, Theory, Research, and Experience*. New York: Academic, 1980.

Prinz, Jesse J. *Gut Reactions: A Perceptual Theory of Emotion*. Oxford: Oxford University Press, 2004.

Rane, D. B. "Good Listening Skills Make Efficient Business Sense." *The IUP Journal of Soft Skills*, Vol. V, No. 4, 2011.

Ray, Satyajit, and Bert Cardullo. *Satyajit Ray: Interviews*. Jackson: University of Mississippi, 2007.

Reagan, Ronald. Speech given after the *Challenger* disaster. *www. historyplace.com/speeches/reagan-challenger.htm*.

Reddick, Ellen. "The importance of body language to your business success." *The Enterprise*. January 19, 2009. 19-25.

Revolutionary Road. Directed by Sam Mendes, 2008. DreamWorks and BBC Studios.

Reynolds, Garr. *Presentation Zen: Simple Ideas on Presentation Design and Delivery*. Berkeley, Calif.: New Riders Pub., 2008.

Rodenburg, Patsy. *The Actor Speaks: Voice and the Performer*. New York: St. Martin's, 2000.

Rodgers, Janet B. *The Complete Voice & Speech Workout: The Documentation and Recording of an Oral Tradition for the Purpose of Training and Practices*. New York: Applause Theatre & Cinema, 2002.

Rogers, Carl R., and F. J. Roethlisberger. "Barriers and Gateways to Communication." *Harvard Business Review*, Vol. 69, No. 6. (Nov. 1991).

Safdar, Saba, Wolfgang Friedlmeier, David Matsumoto, Seung Hee Yoo, Catherine T. Kwantes, Hisako Kakai, and Eri Shigemasu. "Variations of Emotional Display Rules within and across Cultures: A Comparison between Canada, USA, and Japan." *Canadian*

Journal of Behavioural Science/Revue Canadienne Des Sciences Du Comportement 41.1 (2009): 1–10.

Sharer, Kevin. "Why I'm A Listener: Amgen CEO Kevin Sharer." *McKinsey Quarterly* (2012): 61–65. Business Source Complete. Web. July 23, 2013.

Shaver, P. R., S. Wu, and J.C. Schwartz (1992). "Cross-cultural similarities and differences in emotion and its representation: A prototype approach." In M.S. Clark (Ed.), *Review of Personality and Social Psychology* (Vol. 13. Emotion, pp. 175–212). Newbury Park, Calif.: Sage Publications.

The Sixth Sense. Director, M. Night Shyamalan. 1999.

Smith, Greg. "An Invitation to Feel." *www2.gsu.edu/~jougms/FSch1.htm.*

Spangler, Lori. "Gender-Specific Nonverbal Communication: Impact for Speaker Effectiveness." *Human Resource Development Quarterly* 6.4 (1995): 409–19.

Sypher, Beverly Davenport, and Robert N. Bostrom, and Joy Hart Seibert. "Listening, Communication Abilities, and Success at Work." *Journal of Business Communication*. September 1989, 26: 293–303.

Sun Tzu. *The Art of War*. Translated by Samuel B. Griffith. London: Oxford University Press, 1971.

"Sweet About Me" from *Lessons to Be Learned* by Gabriella Cilmi, 2008. Universal Island Records.

Tufte, Edward R. *Beautiful Evidence*. Cheshire, Conn.: Graphics, 2006.

———. "PowerPoint Is Evil." *Wired Magazine. www.wired.com/wired/archive/11.09/ppt2.html.*

Van Der Gaag, Christiaan, Ruud B. Minderaa, and Christian Keysers. "Facial Expressions: What the Mirror Neuron System Can and Cannot Tell Us." *Social Neuroscience* 2.3 (2007): 179–222.

Vivekananda, Swami. "The Great Teachers of the World." Lecture delivered at the Shakespeare Club, Pasadena, California, February 3, 1900. Text available at: *www.ramakrishnavivekananda.info/vivekananda/volume_4/lectures_and_discourses/the_great_teachers_of_the_world.htm.*

Williams, James D. *An Introduction to Classical Rhetoric: Essential Readings*. Chichester, United Kingdom: Wiley-Blackwell, 2009. 210.

Wordsworth, William. "Preface to Lyrical Ballads." *www.bartleby.com/39/36.html.*

Zaremba, Alan Jay. *Speaking Professionally: Influence, Power, and Responsibility at the Podium.* Armonk, N.Y.: M.E. Sharpe, 2012. 187.

Zhu, Jing, and Paul Thagard. "Emotion and Action." *Philosophical Psychology* 15.1 (2002): 19–36.

Index

About the Author

Vikas Gopal Jhingran is the 2007 World Champion of Public Speaking. An MIT-trained engineer and researcher, Vikas suffered from poor speaking skills, due in large part to being an introvert and an immigrant. He studied public speaking to improve in this area and eventually won the Toastmasters 2007 World Championship of Public Speaking. He is the first Indian and only the second person of Asian origin to do so.

Vikas manages a team of engineers at Shell Oil Company and uses his leadership and communication skills to help deliver large projects. He also uses his unique, emotion-driven approach to deliver keynote speeches and conduct workshops that help others become better speakers. He lives with his wife and two sons in Houston, Texas. Visit Vikas's Website at *www.vikasjhingran.com*.